CHARACTERS IN VERSE

poetry *Pt* today

CHARACTERS IN VERSE

Edited by
Rebecca Mee

First published in Great Britain in 1999 by Poetry
Today, an imprint of
Penhaligon Page Ltd, Remus House, Coltsfoot Drive,
Peterborough. PE2 9JX

A Catalogue record for this book is available from the
British Library

ISBN 1 86226 513 5

Typesetting and layout, Penhaligon Page Ltd, England
Printed and bound by Forward Press Ltd, England

Foreword

Characters In Verse is a compilation of poetry, featuring some of our finest poets. This book gives an insight into the essence of modern living and deals with the reality of life today. We think we have created an anthology with a universal appeal.

There are many technical aspects to the writing of poetry and *Characters In Verse* contains free verse and examples of more structured work from a wealth of talented poets.

Poetry is a coat of many colours. Today's poets write in a limitless array of styles: traditional rhyming poetry is as alive and kicking today as modern free-verse. Language ranges from easily accessible to intricate and elusive.

Poems have a lot to offer in our fast-paced 'instant' world. Reading poems gives us an opportunity to sit back and explore ourselves and the world around us.

Contents

Return To Peace

On a Welsh mountain, lush and green
I've left my heart and thoughts serene,
with sloping fields all grazed by sheep,
woolly and white,
I dreamt of Heaven in my sleep;
cosy in our solid little house,
approached through red mud, tracks
and gates,
I thought but little of our fates.

Building on deep dreams of peace,
with plans and hopes of a future;
not just of ease,
brought about by honest work,
creatively providing simple needs.

These things are now just part of my past,
half remembered through a vague haze
of disconsolation,
because we tried to do too much, too soon,
and now these last few years, for me
have been wasted, perhaps,
feeling rejected, with my deepest strengths
unspent, as yet, perhaps.

Malcolm Firth Clark

My Eight Brothers And Four Sisters

I remember when we were small,
How we'd run and play,
You were so special even then,
I've known it every day.

You're the part of my world,
That means so very much,
Always looking out for me,
And with your special touch.

Days have trickled by,
And times flown into years,
Yet we're still together,
Facing all our fears.

Recently we had a party,
And everything was great,
My family is what I treasure,
My thoughts don't hesitate.

I've tried to say how much I love you,
I hope I've made my feelings clear,
I'm here for you now and always,
Because to me you're all so very dear.

All my love always

Chris

Christine Helen Cruse

My Soul Thanks You (My Mentor)

You helped me in times of darkness
I know our paths will never cross
But you are my light on a dark day,
You first appeared to me in a dream
Or so it seemed,
Messages or illusions
There's no magic in saying
You were the dream weaver.

You showed me things I never
Would have seen
My true self has shone through
All down to you,
Love, peace, flowers, future
Anything that helps a rainy day
Have helped me to look up to
Another way.

Painting a picture for the world
Just in the hope to communicate
That's what it's all about, is that my fate?
I guess I will never know
I'm just going to continue to grow.

I can't thank you ever more.
For you are my mentor.

Chris Lombard

Memories Of An Old Lady

As I sit besides my cold fire,
It crackles in the gloom of the dimly lit room,
But it matters not to a lonely old lady,
As I sit waiting for death!

I begin to remember in my distant past,
The old black range I polished so often,
How I baked my bread and cakes for my hungry children,
Sad-mall, Current-cake, Oven-bottoms, they all tasted so well!

On hand and knees at the front doorstep,
Donkey stone in hand, the colour of sand,
How the step is looking grand at the door,
Must not show that we are ever so poor!

Rag and Bone man he would call, as he clattered down the street,
'Any Old Rags, Any Old Rags, Any-Any Old Rags! He would sing,
'Rags for Donkey stones or Dolly - Blues!' He would cry,
As his old horse pulled his cart down the cobbled street.

Charlie Chaplin, Laurel and Hardy on at the pictures,
Three Stooges, oh how they did make us laugh,
Them fine young men, with their shiny hair,
And Pin stripe suits, with spats to match!

Now I sit besides the fireside, my children all grown up,
Grandchildren come and make their noise,
But I can not hear, for what they don't know,
I'm just a little deaf, my dear!

Now my baby boys have all grown up, ever so well,
How their lives will go, I just can't tell,
So now that my work is done, I'll close my eyes,
For now at last, it's time for me to rest.

Barry Cregg

Remembrance Day

The old soldier marches proudly
Thinking of his comrades in war;
In his mind war rages loudly
And in his soul a battle scar.

His mind focused on the past,
He marches with spectres of men,
Bodies destroyed by the blast
Of shellfire in the Ardenne.

But they live on in his mind
Among the skeletons of trees,
Old age they will never find
As gunsmoke drifts on the breeze.

J D Bailey

A Truly Good Friend

I've known my mate for years and years
We've been through much, we've shed the tears
We've helped each other in times of stress
And never a moment has our friendship meant less

It gives me strength when I think of Jayne
Especially on days when I feel grief and pain
We may be miles and miles apart
But that doesn't matter. She's deep in my heart.

And when we're both in a very good mood
We can be quite raucous and sometimes quite rude
We're out for a laugh. We want a good time
And on occasions we tend to go over the line

But that's us. We're one of a kind
And friends like us are hard to find
We accept each other as we are
And that's why we're on an equal par

I love my friend with all my heart
And I try not to think of the day we'll part
I'll enjoy her warmth, and her friendship true
And I'll accept the things she wants to do

I'll tell her now she's my little star
Who shines and sparkles in skies afar
She gives me hope, she makes me see
How lucky I am to have her in me.

Deborah Krueger

Patricia

Patricia my very sincere and thoughtful friend.
No words can ever comprehend.
Her life last autumn was taken away.
To come to terms with leaves me in dismay.
But then I have memories of a special kind.
Holidays hobbies to say the least.
Tim and Susie her feline friends
Brought her more happiness and a life of zest.
Never a grumble a smiling face and
Ready to help. A quality seldom seen
In these days of self, self.
To her memory she so bravely fought.
The cause of which I uphold and support.
Great joy I obtain, although sad.
Patricia was the best friend I ever had.

Mabel Nickholds

Dear Jackie

Do you remember those wild birthday parties?
With us all dressed up to the nines.
Long dresses and make up all over our faces,
As we sat at the table to dine.
Jimmy Shand playing loudly from the old record player.
George the toddler dressed up in a kilt,
Dad and Mum shouting upstairs to turn the noise down
We cried 'Yes' and returned to the lilt.

Do you remember the nights watching football?
Playing badminton up at Aboyne.
The day Wolfie gave me a terrible fright,
And you found me stuck half up a tree.
Laughing at me as George's bike fell to bits,
His mudguards tied up with my laces.
I can see it so clearly just like yesterday,
Special people and favourite places.

Do you remember those nights at the discos?
Adam Ant was your favourite star.
The night the Police dropped us off at the Kerloch,
When I locked the keys in the car,
Or the night up at Ballater when the car wouldn't start,
Waking up half the neighbourhood.
With our high heeled shoes and the noise of our laughter
We left as quick as we could.

Dear Jackie, I Thank you for always being there,
For the fun and the laughter and showing you care.
Thank you for the memories I treasure do dearly,
Good Health and best wishes I send you sincerely.

Pat Lawson

Unseen Visions

When the clocks have turned,
and the world has unwined,
the trees grown old,
and mists roll on behind.

I will stand on this mountain top,
and look back on my ways,
seeing all the things I have done,
along the road in my days.

And when I see a cloudy patch,
of some sad time,
let me look now upon what is mine,
I have a beautiful vision of this
beautiful land,
resting here now, asleep, under my
hand,
and she returns my thoughts as she lies
here in awe,
and looks now with me on all the things
I saw,
but we're together now, so I know how to smile,
and lie here in peace with her, just a little while!

Roy Gavin

The Beauty Of Marguerite

(Dedicated to my best friend, My sister Marguerite Steng)

The fiery spirit that is oh so Contraire,
The smouldering passions held within a heartbeat,
That's the tempting allure of the mysterious Marguerite.

Her eyes of deep blue hold questions unanswered,
Don't ask, she won't say, she'll only retreat,
Deep into self and the world of Marguerite.

Vivacious and fun and such a great mover,
She'd sparkle and sing her full repertoire complete,
Men would be dazzled by the spell of Marguerite.

A lively and fiery spirit, tempered only by love,
Devotion to children, family, a giver of treats,
That's the generous heart of my soul mate Marguerite.

Her fire and her spirit jaded only by time,
Her moods and her passions now a little deplete,
But still their lurks a flame, The beauty Marguerite.

Beauty shines within us and never to be lost,
Not age or illness nor times rhythmic beat,
Can ever dim or shade the Beauty of Marguerite.

Floreine McIntyre

11

Tribute To A Saint - Mary My Friend

I met a lady some few years ago
  Of steadfast eyes and vehement in speech.
In her tender years she made to God a vow
  That of Jesus she would spend her life to teach.
She never wavered from the path she trod,
  Because the vow was made unto her God.

Her fruitful life had many hilly patches,
  Not often were there roses at her door;
Still love shone through in numerous shining batches.
  Through suffering she would serve her Lord the more.
She never wavered from the path she trod,
  Because the vow was made unto her God.

Her depth of love for Jesus was profound,
  No earthly charm could draw her love away.
In His dear service all her life was bound,
  Though fragile in human state, she still could pray.
She never wavered from the path she trod,
  Because the vow was made unto her God.

She had her human traits, but who can't own?
  His mercy and His grace would prove her worth,
Let he that is without, cast the first stone.
  From the beginning her faith had given birth;
She never wavered from the path she trod,
  Because the vow was made unto her God.

She felt His nearness more on lonely days
And longed to be with Him, to end her quest.
Then nearing the end of life's chaotic maze
He straightened out the path for His dear guest.
She never wavered from the path she trod,
The vow was now made perfect by her God.

Doreen Barwell

Remembering Friends

Good friendship is a great gift to receive,
Sometimes a stranger comes along -
And they give you this priceless legacy!
Without knowing what they have done,
Maybe, You of all people -
Have trusted and loved someone very dearly,
But in the end there was nothing!
Nothing at all!
So you build a wall around you,
Too afraid to be hurt again,
Then someone with a cherry 'Hello'
A ready laugh and a lovely smile,
And the healing begins, bit by bit.
Hope stirs in that person's heart again.
Yet, these friendly people do not realise,
Just what miracle they are performing.
Friends come and go through a lifetime,
They all leave their mark, good and bad.
Yet this hand of friendship,
Is valued very highly indeed,
Yes! Good friendship is the greatest gift of all!

Margaret Pearce

A Brother

The laughter's gone, the voice is stilled
no more the funny jest.
So many dreams lay unfulfilled
all plans are laid to rest.

A brother's guiding knowledge
sixty years, and more I've known.
Advice so sound and stable
as through the years we've grown.

The memories of our childhood
so clear now in my mind.
Of cricket and of fishing
and bird nests we would find.

He worked so hard at Grammar School
and left me way behind.
Those books he'd read stayed with him
most answers he could find.

Our love of classic music
not for us the modern sounds.
His love of English countryside
and wildlife knew no bounds.

In life there's now an empty space
that nothing else can fill.
For someone's gone away now
I miss him, and always will.

Alan J Vincent

Friendship

(For Janet: a special friend)

To honour your friend and respect all their fears,
Extend the same welcome to laughter and tears,
To listen to them with your eyes and your heart,
Acknowledge their pain, and set them apart
As a person you value, a person you love,
A fellowship granted from God up above.

To be willing to silently sit by their side,
Forsaking your needs as in you they confide,
To pray with them and for them and never to judge,
To seek out suggestions and now and then nudge,
To hug them and heal with the touch of your hand,
Consider their feelings, and then understand.

To share all their hopes and their dreams in full trust,
To know when to talk and when 'be still' you must.

To show that you value them 'just as they are'
And give them the freedom to follow their star.
To journey with them as they seek out God's will
And never to mind when the path is uphill.

Such is a friendship which money can't buy -
As close as a heartbeat, as free as the sky:
Scripted in heaven, by God's hand 'tis penned.

A wonderful friendship.

Thank you, my friend.

Pat Marsh

The Gift

No matter how far apart we are,
you're never far away.
Because you're here in my mind,
each and every day.
And when I think of you,
I think of how we laugh.
You help to make life's winding road,
a much straighter path.
No amount of money
could buy a gift like this.
But the gift of friendship
is one that everybody should give.

Rachel C Zaino

Tape For A Dead Man

Broad, wide and strong
A God in his mind,
He relaxed like the death of Chatterton
Smothered by an auburn light
As sound came organic
From a hidden CD
Barely there in his mind,
Lead eyed and stoic,
Rolling;
Time stopped in the room
Nothing moved
His body, inside
Rushed away
Getting weaker
Aware, focused
But naive and unaware of how rapid
'Kev . . .' he spoke
' . . . I can tell you've smoked a hell of a lot of dope'
Wasted for leisure,
Wasting away in time
What happened to the years
We all expected?
Broad and Strong.

Kevin Rolfe

Appreciation

I would just like to thank you,
For being there when I needed you.
When I was upset, and thought
That nobody seemed to care,
I turned around
And you were there.
When there seemed to be
No easy way out,
You came along
And helped me out.
When I needed you most
You stuck by me,
Took me in your arms
And lifted me to calmer seas.
And so I would like to thank you,
For being my friend
And showing it in the things you do.

Karen McLaughlin

Sojourn

*(For my late father, who always enjoyed family
holidays in the Norfolk countryside)*

The springtime of our lives is here,
The days are long, and filled with cheer,
Youth gives its own lengthening of the days,
So much to do, sing, laugh, praise,
The country walk, when we heard the cuckoo,
Was many years ago, summer days
Were carefree, as we returned home,
Suitcases in the hall, letters on the mat.
We drank our tea in the garden.
Washed our clothes, and stroked the cat,
Then, with the holiday over, we went back to work,
No more time to sit around and shirk,
A week later, we collected our holiday snaps.
As time went by, illness came along,
We found ourselves standing by the graveside,
Then, a few years on, realisation,
That some things are gone.
That same photograph, now in a frame,
Stands gazing down on me,
As I play a waiting game.

Jane Owen

Goodbye Blues

How sad I am that you have gone away
But in my heart is where you will stay
Your constant pain could not be kept at bay
Glad I met you; I'll not regret that day

I remember your beauty and your wit
Clothes, hair and even the way you used to sit
I talk to you and wonder if you hear
I miss your laughter and would like you near

Your humour was so rare as it was never cruel
Your smile was always quick, you were a jewel
About heaven, there is something I must know
Is there late night shopping and shall we go?

E Chaplin

Our House - Sightings

This was my mother's and father's house
and now it is mine to live in.
Past; From the kitchen window I catch sight of
My father, shirtless, sun-roasting
wheeling his loaded barrow down the crazy paving
to his greenhouse.
As I come down the stairs I catch sight of
My mother peeling fresh vegetables for Sunday dinner.
I hear her whistling her favourite tune -
'Around the world, I've searched for you,'
I sit in the lounge watching TV and catch sight of
My grandmother walking across the back lawn
on her way to retrieve her bone-dry washing.
All three of them walk the paths, climb the stairs,
shut the doors, just leave the room,
encircle this building with their glimpsed presence.

Present; The robin still sits roundly on the linepost my
father installed.
The crimson rhododendrons my mother planted
continue to flower in fiery mood.
The laburnum my grandmother insisted be
radically pruned, has regrown spectacularly.
My cat sniffs the concrete paths with interest
following past scents of football and labourings.
Of times of celebration when we all gathered
to witness the markings of their lives' passage.
Now, only I keep a relative vigil
eager to maintain elusive sightings of them all.

Future; My son in time will watch for
Sightings of me . . . with them . . . in this his house.

Geraldinne Berrisford

Blue

You lay your head upon my knee
With big brown eyes gaze up at me.
Warm eyes that love so trustingly
Stout heart that beats so loyally.
What truer friend could I desire
What qualities could more admire
Than those you always bring to me
So eager and so willingly.
A love that never questions why
A love that's mine until you die.
Oh who could ever wish for more.
A cold wet nose, a friendly paw.
A tail that wags incessantly
A shadow never leaving me.
They say that animals are dumb
They know you're not my faithful chum.
You look at me and I can see
Just what you're thinking silently.
Somehow you always seem to know
When I am feeling sad and low
And then you gently lick my hand
As though you really understand.
You never want to leave my side
Gaze up at me with so much pride.
I could not bear to part with you
You mean so much to me dear Blue.

Sadly you had to go to sleep
And now a lonely vigil keep.
But though you are no longer here
I always sense you very near.

J D Winchester

Old Friends

In green fields let me run again and feel the sun upon my brow,
and let us be as one again, not far apart, as we are now.
Then let the joy course through my blood and let the bubbling
laughter rise . . .
let youth's first spring renew my blood and see the world through
wondering eyes.

Our skies were always blue my friend, the winds of life were always
warm . . .
of Time itself there was no end; our ships could weather every
storm . . .
The hours we spent are not forgot, engraved in mem'ry they shall be,
for friendship was our blessed lot, and shall be for eternity.

That wide-faced, knowing, cocky grin, that questioning but impish
look
that seemed to take the whole world in, with life itself the open
book.
We trod the fields, we walked the lanes, we shared the lows and then
the highs,
we had our losses, and our gains - thus strengthened we our close-
bound ties.

There is no real tomorrow then, for slowly night pales into day . . .
and then we find 'remember when' is only just a thought away.
And so the numbered years have passed, for Time's not one to drag
his feet -
yet soon or late, t'will come at last, when once more two old friends
will meet,

For Tom.

Ken Allen

Lines For My Sister

Not a cross word was said outside the sanatorium,
But tears were shed or parried
As her corpse to the crematorium
In a vale of sorrow we carried.

Death's procession makes a start;
The family begins to crumble;
One by one we must depart,
Ashes to ashes, dust to dust; soon, a rumble.

'Have faith,' the vicar said,
'We shall all one day meet again.' A prayer?
Somewhere, some place among the dead.
In the meantime, the grief is hard to bear.

To nothingness, in a great void,
To a great silence we shall go.
O cruel sentence we cannot avoid!
The thought of this makes us grieve so!

We were with her silently praying
In love's companionship and hope.
Not alone was she in her going;
Though alone she walked that final slope.

It took a certain boldness
To cross over in such style.
Her parting, despite its sadness,
Will be remembered in her smile.

Angus Richmond

My Friend Jesus

The one I love is Jesus,
My love for Him is deep,
The reason why I love Him,
My soul I know He'll keep.

We'll travel the way together,
He is certain of the road,
And when I get so weary
I know He'll share my load.

I am happy in His service,
I'll serve Him every day,
Then at last He'll call me,
In heaven with Him to stay.

W C Niel

Janice

Early morning, bus stop.
On the way to work.
Beehive hairdo, mohair coat.
Pencil slim black skirt.
We reached our destination.
Bells began to ring.
We worked for the same company.
And I took her 'neath my wing.
I, was twenty-two, she was just sixteen.
But, over forty years of friendship,
We've closed the gap between.
What larks we've had together
We twisted, rocked and rolled.
We both found loving husbands,
And took on the band of gold.
Sometimes we were miles apart.
She lived three years in Paris.
Where her husband was employed.
We thought our friendship fated,
So we were overjoyed,
When she returned to England,
We picked up where we left off,
And we only changed one thing,
She's fifty-eight, I'm sixty-four,
Now I'm tucked beneath *her* wing.

Brenda Söhngen

Friendship

It started with a popstar and his fan club, long ago,
I picked her name from many and thought I'd have a go.
Her hobbies were the same as mine, we must be kindred minds,
Who would have thought this friendship would stand the test of
time?

We wrote for years, though living near, never thought to meet,
Our hopes and wishes, daily grind all written on news sheets.
One time we met, it wasn't right, our conversation stilted,
(Much better that we write our thoughts, we don't want friendship
wilted).

Each moved their homes, a new address, but still the letters flowed.
A boyfriend, then a marriage, a move away - she glowed!
A son, then two, the years soon passed, my sons went through their
phases
Of motorbikes and girlfriends, living in different places.

Letters filled with sadness as parents left this world,
Letters filled with gladness as relationships unfurled.
One marriage, then another, grandchildren now appeared,
The years still tried our friendship as retirements drew near.

Throughout the years we kept our faith, each month a page or two,
Keeping in touch with each other's lives, and so our friendship grew.
Both now are in their sixties, and still the tale goes on
A friendship, deep and lasting until our days are done.

Vi Robinson

Souvenir

Newhaven; a dawn break,
the last croissant shared.
Wistful smiles, pangs of heartache,
as we both remember.

My blue eyes, below
yours lustrously green.
Edelweiss, alpine meadows,
lavender King and Queen.

Our brief reign in the sun
aboard eagle's broad wings,
uplifted as one,
souls soared, somersaulting.

On the ferry, clouds' shadows,
insidious rain,
porthole view streaked and shrouded,
stranded tears at the pane.

Bittersweet sugared coffee,
awake after a dream;
can't re-bottle the Genie
or the heated drink's steam.

So I absorb the full flavour,
find fresh peace in this place,
precious seconds to savour
as I gaze at your face.

Ian Newman

Odd Ode To Jim

Wakey wakey rise and shine
For thy bed though must not pine
Have you heard 'tis sad but true
To sleep doth make a man feel new.

But thou must get up and go to work
So take thy bed don't be a jerk
And whence arrive upon it lie
Go man go and don't be shy.

And dream of how to hammer the nails
Into the wood when all else fails
And when thy finds thy's in a plight
Get up man and put out the light.

And when thou finds thy've hit thy thumb
Those impolite words must be rum
Enough to send the sparks fly high
And thou collapse with one big sigh.

Just to think how lucky thou will be
To find thy bed beneath thy knee
Big sighs of joy be heard the more
For thou won't have to fall on floor.

Joan Vincent

Friendship

I always feel better when I see you,
It's not how you look, but the things that you do.
A friend so treasured in you I found,
My ego is boosted by you, when I'm down.
Reassurance when I'm in doubt,
Admonishment when rules I flout.
I always feel better when we meet,
My secrets divulged, your replies discreet.
A hand to hold, a shoulder to cry on, a sympathetic ear,
The advice you give always fills me with cheer.
Where would we be without our friends?
Loyalty, trust, are not fashion trends,
That friendly hand one has to earn,
As we travel through life, this, we all learn.

Patti Ryall

A Celebration Of Friendship

We are gathered here tonight
  Because we are friends.
Some we've known for many years,
Some have even dried our tears.

Others have encouraged us
  With words to lead us on,
When life was dark and lonely
And everything seemed wrong.

Yet through the days of darkness
We've been privileged to share
The perfect love of Jesus
With friends who really care.

Dear friends, we are bound together always
  By the love of Christ our Lord,
  The unseen Friend, who listens
  To our weak and trembling word.

So let's rejoice in knowing Him
Give thanks for each new day
And pray that He may be to us
The closest, dearest Friend of all.

Praise be to His Holy Name
  For evermore.

Amen.

B J Evans

May

You were short and stocky,
Fair hair, in small bun,
Complexion pink and white.

People called you
'The saint of Jericho',*
Intelligent, sensitive,
Impish sense of humour,
Everybody's friend.

You walked many miles
With Blackie, Labrador-cross.
You knew birds, plants, animals,
Always in harmony
With your surroundings.

You had true beauty -
Shining out from within you,
Joyous smile of greeting
When we met on our walks.

Now in the Parks,
Where you walked Blackie,
Grow three hawthorn trees,
Flowers red, pink, and white,
As your memorial.

May, you were such
A truly special person.
It was my privilege
To know you, and Blackie,
And to be your friend.

*A district of Oxford

Maria-Christina

Stewart's Hibiscus

Every year and in their season,
Its blooms abide the plan,
The work of a God incarnate,
Shared briefly with a man.

With Surgeon's knife, some healing tape,
And tools to aid the bee,
He added to the master plan,
For you and I to see -

A 'single' and a 'double pink',
A 'red' and 'red and white',
Altogether stemming from 'one'
Hibiscus of delight.

Every year and in their season,
Its blooms abide the plan,
And heighten our remembrance of
A much loved 'gentle' man.

Bill Scovell

Daniel

Daniel was three,
Fair-haired and bright eyed,
A bundle of inexhaustible fun,
An ever smiling friend,
A loveable toddler,
A child of open spaces,
Of heather moorland and fell,
Lakeland tarns and the roaring sea.

Daniel loved to walk,
To climb to soaring heights,
To run in the wind,
To splash in inviting puddles,
To shout to the birds in flight.
Hand in hand, we climbed,
The mountain peak, beckoning us.
Then he paused, lost deep in thought.

And when he spoke,
His childlike utterance,
Brought tears to my eyes.
I know what to say to Jesus,
When we meet Him.
Daniel was looking,
At where hill and heaven met.
A few weeks later, a crashed car,
On a country road,
Gave Daniel, his chance,
To step from hilltop into heaven,
And to say, 'I love you Jesus',
As he met His God.

Brenda Gill

Valentine

I must send my love
A valentine
That card will do -
It looks just fine
It's big
With ribbons . . . heart . . .
And costs a lot
It should my status
Make quite hot!

So murmur men
Full hypnotised
By rows of cards . . .
Ain't Valentine's Day
Commercialised?

Your card
Which I didn't *Have* to buy
Contains no heart or ribbons . . .
I wonder why?
It cost only a quid or so
(Pretty cheap as they go!)
But you surely sense me well enough
To know
That
In My book
The important thing
Is the Love and Care
The Choosing took
For I want this little card
To say
'I Love You More And More
Each Day.'

For *This sentiment*
Is
I do opine
The *True* meaning
Of The Valentine.

John Crowe

Birthday Memories

Your Birthday has come round once again but you are no longer
                                                              here
I try to hide my heartache but the pain I am unable to bare
The many times I've needed you and the many tears I've cried
God knows how much I needed you so why did he let you die
I cannot give you a Birthday card or give a gift to you
So I lay these flowers on your grave there's nothing left to do
I read the inscription on your grave I read it through my tears
I know you still watch over me you didn't want to leave
But the Angels came and took you Mam I wish I knew the reason
                                                             why
He took you when I wasn't there and didn't let me say goodbye
I would give all the world to have you back just to have you here
                                                          with me
They say God only takes the best and I know this must be true
For of all the Mothers in the world none could compare to you
I long to have you back Mam I need you here with me
But time goes on instead of back so I know it cannot be
So all you who has a Mother love her while you may
Because when you are without her you'll feel as I do today.

Christine Isaac

First Love

Lone footprints in the sand
      Where once were more
            Indented by the score
Then, life was still unplanned
      And we as children saw
            Our empires on the shore
Built by our youthful band

Friends we were and stayed
      Until life for all
            Did hollow echo call
And to transient realms we strayed
      But two did fall
            Into lover's sacred hall
Where cherished bonds we made

Lone footprints in the sand
      Where once we trod
            With buoyant feet unshod
Juxtaposed, safe, hand in hand
      Then as adults we did plod
            Bore no optimistic rod
No gilded Promised Land

Friends we were and stayed
      Though far apart
            Each fragile tender heart
Had to its kismet played
      Fated from the start
            This youthful love did smart
And the drama's now in shade.

G Carpenter

To Nick

Dreams stir the soul,
Memories of touch and comfort
in tears and parting,
and times past pleasures.
A longing for you near
in music messages
last heard together.
  'Remember me,
  you who live there -
  you were once
  a true love of mine.'

  Pamela Courtney

To A Distant Friend

You may be many hundred miles away,
But in my heart you are always close to me.
We may not meet for many a long day,
But in my mind's eye I can always see
The friend whom I have always held so dear;
Whose friendship was so special from the start:
That special bond we have still keeps you near,
And gives me comfort while we are apart.

Eleanor Lynn

Friendship

When in sorrow or pain we reach out for a friend.
To share with us our fears once again.

But who do we need when we're full of joy.
It may be the birth of a baby boy
Or any other great delight.
A friend can keep your future bright.

Share with you your worries and fears,
Calm your nerves and dry your tears.

Laugh with you and share happy days,
Solve your problems in many ways.

Say not a word when anger is nigh,
But turn away with a look or a sigh.

Sends flowers whenever the occasion arises,
Telephones when needed and is full of surprises.

Friendship that lasts from youth to old age,
Like a book to be read from first to last page.

Pamela Bryan

New Friends

The telephone rang loud and clear,
I said hello who is it there,
A friendly voice replied to me,
I rang your number just to see,
If you could help me find a friend,
My other one has met her end.
Her time has come to say goodbye,
I'm left alone to sit and cry,
These empty hours I cannot face,
I need a friend to fill the space,
The loneliness goes on and on,
Now that my doggy friend has gone.
She needed help there was no doubt,
I had to help this lady out.
A friend she'd found, she rang to say,
Now we've been friends since that first day.

Jan Murray

Not Too Young To Die
(For Judith)

I am not too young to die;
Not I;
As young as that dear friend
Buried a week ago.
I see her
Brilliant in the radiant sunshine
Of an Italian afternoon.
She is no more
So before
The bell tolls for me
And you
Let us run under the sweeping winter clouds
On a deserted beach;
Dance, we still can, the night away
In a teenage discothèque;
Stretch our willing, capable bodies
To the limit;
Walk with firm, fast step
By the riverside
And revel in the beauty
Our eyes can still perceive.
Don't let us lose
The Love of laughter,
Become too serious to joke,
Despise an innocent prank
Or hesitate to jump for joy
For simple pleasures,
Forget a friend lost, friendship enduring.

Frances Gillian Petroni

Brief Encounter

For a brief time I lost all train of thought
As you approached the bar. And by the bye,
It was not me but Phillip's help you sought
And patient stood until you caught his eye,
Then waited while he mixed the drink you bought
To savour liquid heaven, golden rye.
Yet his was not the only eye you caught —
Mine too, and as the spider can't deny
His urge to love black widow, be consort,
Although he almost certainly will die,
Could I resist such silken strands spun taut?
I came to where you sat — oh me, oh my.

So beauteous, you, in black and scarlet clad,
No hungry widow poised insatiate.
From carmined lips a smile to make me glad
That I'd escaped the hapless consort's fate,
Retained my life though lost my heart — I'm mad,
I fell headlong for Venus incarnate.
Poor mortal, I, this errant Galahad
Dared court a dream, became infatuate
But time destroyed what little time we had,
The hours for all their minutes would not wait.
One final smile so infinitely sad
Then you were gone to meet your waiting date.

Ashley Morton-Cameron

My Family

My family has put themselves out
For me, when times I needed
They didn't ask or tell or give advice
Just support me 'til I succeeded

Their door is always open
The tea is in the pot
A room is ready clean and tidy
Until my need I have not got

To thank them seems impossible
As I have often tried
A word a gift a telephone call
My family, is my pride

From the youngest to the elder
They're all the same to me
My family is so special
I want the world to see

Anita Mercer

Affirmation

One's friends are always beautiful,
As children are.
The vow of love's the same, perhaps,
Though not the same
The fierce fine filter of our view.
  That is more true;
Each friend I have has, had,
  Her, his own beauty, non-pareil.

And its account is lodged in my heart's vault.

A stance, a steady
Look, a turn, a toss of head.
Quick light in the eyes,
A firm hand to my grip, yet still
A willingness
To draw a different bead
Upon the angle of our thought.

This, which is beauty, knows not rot nor age.

- Not so the perfect lines of eyebrow, lip and nose -
(We never, friends, had those!)
  Now halting, hesitating we
Grow crumpled, wizened, ash-grey, dull
  Of eye, our hearing all off-key.

And some have fled from their frail cage,
My dear, my dears.

  The body's death is triviality.
The quintessential spirit does not change.

For all the days that are my lot
Your beauty stays untouched, untinged.
  The glint, the lift,
The lyre-note from within

Are our sure signs of immortality.
Amen.

Margaret Braddock

Matthew Mark

There was an old man who lived in a tree
As to why was a mystery to me
So I asked him quite civily 'Is it nice up there?'
And he chuckled and said 'Well, it's full of fresh air'
'How long' I asked 'Have you lived on that branch?'
'Since I lost my way home from the Rotary Dance
I took the first right and walked straight ahead
But the end of the road was the end that was dead'
'So why did you stay and not turn around?'
'Well I liked what I saw, both the trees and the ground
They were green and lush and the leaves were unfurled
So I decided to move in and up in the world'
'But what do you do in the winter?' I asked
'When the leaves are all gone and the limbs are unmasked'
'Well I just move next door' he pointed 'dear sir
That tree's always green, it's an aged conifer'
Now, it's been many a year that old Matthew Mark
Has lived up those trees on the edge of the park
The locals all know him and ply him with beer
To keep him quite happy and full of good cheer
But I know that one day he'll fall dead from his tree
And we'll stand and remember Matthew Mark RIP

Ann B Rogers

Life Goes On

At one of life's crossroads you'll take the wrong turn,
Mistakes must be made before you can learn.
That life can be cruel as well as kind,
And the bridges you burn you must now leave behind.
But I find myself at an all time low
Knowing my mistake was letting you go.
The words you once whispered I no longer hear
I miss your touch, the taste of your tears.

Like a guiding star above the sea of love, you led me safe to shore,
Like an open fire on a stormy night you made me feel secure.
Like a ray of sun on a frosty morn you'd melt my fears away,
Like a sinner outside the gates of heaven I fall to my knees and pray
That one day I'll feel your love again
To share the laughs, to comfort the pain.

But deep down I know that day won't come
No words can undo the damage that's done.
But given one wish, I'd wish for it to be,
To turn back time to when it was just you, and me.

But the hands of time, well as you know,
They never falter, never slow,
The seconds fall one by one
As faithful as the setting sun.

So here I stand head hung in shame
With no one but myself to blame
For although not blind I failed to see
How much you really meant to me.

But like a broken mirror upon the floor
Once shattered we must reflect no more
Mistakes like glass must be swept away
As life goes on, or so they say.

Stuart McBarron

Sister And Friend

No-one could replace her my sister, friend
Remember childhood fights and rows not new
Always there to see me through good times bad
You never forget your true best reliable sad
It seems now a distant memory I had
      I miss you now

Take away the flowers they're not needed now
You're gone to a special place I can't go how
All my life we were a family so close
Until the tight of my life my special sister
Whatever you did a glow we couldn't resist
      Memories all mine

A special place is a far-away star
We look skywards it's not so far
Why is life one minute laughter then tears
It should for you have lasted many years
Your family the missing chair a link
A missing part of life's family jigsaw
      You are all

Take care of her she deserves so much
Our far away sister still no special touch
Please if you could always remember love
A thousand embraces of feelings you above
Our eyes always blinking tears can't hide
      A peaceful find
My sister always in our hearts like treasure
      Nothing you measure.

Bridie Moody

Eileen

She passed away one summer's day some twenty years ago
Yet I can still recall her face and I still miss her so.
Her dark hair, short and loosely waved, her eyes of gentle brown,
Her happy smile, her cheery wave; she didn't often frown.

Our daughters went to Playgroup and that was where we met.
She was the Playgroup Leader. I never shall forget
The time she taught us dancing beneath a Maypole bright.
She'd made the pole from toilet rolls but it got damp overnight!

Just when all the children had round the Maypole sped
The damp and soggy loo rolls collapsed upon their heads!
The pretty ribbons all were spoiled. Her hard work came to naught
But I knew the children loved her. Love like that isn't bought.

She knew where migrant geese made nests along a hidden brook.
We had to be so very still before she'd let us look.
She showed us purple orchids in the water meadows there
And every plant she knew by name and each bird in the air.

The last time that I saw her she was learning how to drive.
Her hands were animated. She was joyously alive.
Next day I had a 'phone call, a neighbour so they said,
Was ringing just to let me know that Eileen was found dead.

Her epilepsy took her. So sudden in the night
A grand mal came upon her and she had no chance to fight.
It's not like some disorders where often there's a warning.
Poor Eileen died at home that night and was not found 'till the
morning.

Yes, even now I miss her though it's been a while since then.
I miss her simple innocence, I miss my gentle friend.
I miss our days together. I miss our country drives.
I want to turn the clock back to when she was alive.
I'm standing at the ironing board and her face appears to me -
She's running by that little brook, she's happy and she's free.

L S Robinson

Mine Host

(In loving memory of Carole [Scottie] who died on 14th September 1992)

My friend walked with me through those learning years
Through the thick and thin, through the laughter and tears.
My friend bore with me through those doubts and fears
Through the breaking hearts, through the applause and cheers.
We laughed so much over silly things
And cried together over the hurt life brings.
I remember well when we were there
I remember her look, I remember her stare.
She always knew the right from wrong,
She saw through the weakness, she made us strong.
But now she's left, gone from this place,
Gone is her laughter, gone is her face.
The hurt stays near, barely locked away,
But, then laughter too can burst astray.
And life goes on, as on it must.
Ashes to ashes and dust to dust.
But whilst I remember my loving friend
She lives with me right to the end.
Her beautiful spirit will never die
She reaches out, her touch, her sigh,
They envelope me when I need her most,
My dearest friend, my long lost host.

Joan Bullock

Blossoms Everlasting

The edelweiss grows high above
the soft and fertile plain
on rocky Alpine summits
near to the heart of God
its pure white bracts
surround a golden heart
young men risk their lives
to gather blooms for sweethearts
who cherish them
not only for their beauty
but as messengers of love

Along life's rocky pathway
people grow like flowers
some brightly coloured, fragrant
bold or shy
prickly perhaps
or wilting
as the years go by

You, my dear friend Ros
are like the edelweiss
a treasure prized

    Betty Hocking

Stolen Moments

Memories of us together still floods my mind,
The thoughts of your love so divine,
When down by the water's edge, we would meet,
An encounter we would always keep,
Precious memories of our walks through the park,
We never thought then that we would ever part,
I think of our first loving kiss,
Those sweet soft lips, that I now miss,
Precious thoughts of your gentle body, laying next to me,
With you I always wanted to be,
Those stolen moments in time, when you were mine,
How could I forget, that moment when our bodies entwined,
Those autumn nights when the stars shone bright,
When we kissed, and held each other in the moon's light,
Your love for me was so perfect and true,
Those stolen moments in time I spent with you,
Then came the time we parted, and said our goodbye,
That feeling of sadness that made us cry,
But now, all I have are the precious memories of you,
Precious memories of a lover, a special friend ever true.

Allan Young

Remembering Friends

Talking of friends, I'd like to say.
I've met nice people along the way
Friends at school, and also at work.
Friends I write to, which I often shirk,
except at Christmas and birthday times
Then a letter enclosed, memories aligned.
A special friend, I've found of late.
Someone I care for, a family mate.
'My daughter' I find, a friend indeed.
Someone to talk to, when there's a need.
I can also listen, when she needs to talk.
And we enjoy the company taking a walk.
'Trouble shared is a trouble halved.'
So we usually end up having a laugh.
Lots of time, we do our own thing.
Then we just give each other a ring.
As life continues, its uncertain path.
I hope my friendships in life, will last.

Pat Rider

Goodbye, My Friend

Lowered into an earthy grave,
The blackness swallowing up what I had known
So short a time before, had claimed as friend.
This - now no more than putrefying clay,
Devoid of sense, of beauty, thought . . .
Deprived of Life -
Condemned forever to abhor the light,
To shelter rather in the arms of Death.
This - this had been You;
That youthful face still seems
To haunt the awful dimness of the night,
Though reason tells me that this cannot be,
For I am here, alive, and you, my friend
Are passing from the cares of yesterday
Into the vacuum of Eternity.

Now, even as I look, the earth begins
To fall; at first quite slowly, then with gathering pace.
The lighter grains are softly trickling in,
To knock with timid touch upon that wall
Of wood encasing your fragility.
You do not wake; nor even when the clods
Begin to fall and cover up from sight
All trace that you were born, have lived, have loved,
Have fought and wrestled, hated, laughed and cried.

Within that shrouded dwelling is interred
Far more than any seeking eye could see;
The shadow of a friendship free conferred,
So, close beside my friend lies - ME.

Brian G Davies

On Reading Unexpectedly The Obituary Of A School Friend

Gently smiling from the printed page
Arnold evoked a distant, wartime age.
His face retained within my memory's cell
The schoolboy features I recalled so well.
Once, we smiled conspiratorially
Across the desk tops of the Spanish class;
The huge, forbidding, 'Dodie' bullied us to pass
With honours on examination day,
But soon there came a parting of the way.
You stayed on. I left the school we knew.
The gap between us very quickly grew
Through years of war, then Academe,
In your case gaining great esteem
From colleagues in your chosen field
Of Medicine; whilst I achieved but modestly,
Those days at school a treasured memory.
The face I met with suddenly today
Recalled a happy friendship
Now sadly passed away.

Walter Simkins

Cadbury

Was he my friend or my daughter's?
We both doted on him
And he generously seemed to love us both.

He was born under her bed,
My daughter's, with a brother and a sister,
And then abandoned by his ma
As soon as he could eat and drink.

He grew to be beautiful
As only a ginger cat can be,
Long haired, gentle,
A perfect furry friend.

He greeted my daughter's return
From school or play,
And walked beside her
With every sign of devotion.

He sunbathed, legless, on the rockery,
Or wooed the goldfish with a soggy paw.
He leapt on errant leaves and grasshoppers
Ever hopeful.

And then he vanished.
One night he vanished.
And all our calling
And all our crying
Did not bring him back.

Ann Harrison

A Butterfly In The Garden

Four sturdy walls
The sun-shire Folly.
The raspberries
And the black-currents' ease.
The mariner short to his tack
Where, once, a friend said,
'I'm leaving and I'm not coming back.'
A letter from that friend;
The dipping flight
Erratic as a 'falling'.
The black-as-night
And purest calling.
Came the solitary: knew grief? -
'Certain-not the raspberry-thief'
Can beauty flaunt?
Without the mirror, daunt?
Dash hopes of 'fitting'?
'I see no sign that 'Poppy' can't!
I see a butterfly and sample flitting . . .'

Robin Sackett

Dawn

I see her only once a week,
She's bright, fair-haired and full of fun.
We have but little time to speak,
She's blue-eyed, slim and very young.

Just in front, her seat she takes,
Then turns and smiles across the aisle.
I sometimes think it's this that makes
My churching Sunday all worthwhile.

Her name she takes from time of day
We call the early morn.
Although I've yet to hear her say
That she was born at dawn.

Reg Renwick

I Feel Pretty

Moving house in the sixties,
And settling children in school
Knowing no-one around me
Invited by neighbour to call;
I met a woman called Laura,
We talked of her sons and my girls -
Traded concerns and made plans.

So much common ground, such instant rapport
Soon welded together with synchronised thought.
'There for each other' before jargon devalued
Its sense, at each end of the phone
Listening, caring. Of homework and housework,
Holidays and tennis, dressmaking, picnics, recipes, et al,
DIY and driving, gardens and church fetes, non-stop chase.

And off to keepfit in nearby lunch class.
Avoiding all glances at motley attending.
Honky tonk piano, plonkety plonk.
Skipping ropes thudding on to the mat.
'I feel pretty-I feel pretty-Da Da Da-da'
Triggering mirth; unstoppable glee
When recalling those days of trying to escape
From teenage angst and its ills.
Still friends.

Jean Greenall

Jan And John -Two Special People

Full of excitement we waited
September would never come it seemed
When we would leave this home of ours
For a holiday beyond our wildest dreams.

We had a wonderful time with you
Every second packed with fun,
Incredible things awaited us,
Round every corner, on the run.

Five states from Texas we travelled
In those two glorious weeks,
From town house, by plane and trailer
To peacefully beautiful mountain retreat.

Unbelievably glorious canyons, all colours
Each with a charm of its own,
A train ride to heaven, a picture show,
Boat trip, horse riding, even a monsoon!

Campfires, picnics and rodeo too.
And incredible sand dunes with a coral pink hue.
We saw so much in those two short weeks
I still can't believe it's all true.

We are so grateful to you, Jan and John
For your generosity and kindness too,
We send more love than is possible
To convey on these pages to you.

Our hearts are full of emotion
How we feel is difficult to show -
We think of you often with fondness and love,
The two biggest hearted people we know.

Maureen Gard

True Friends

True friends are gold, by the handful,
that shine in the small change of life.
They will outlast the bloodiest strife,
to laugh over battles quite awful
when, later, glasses you pour full
and relive the stabs of the knife.
True friends are gold, by the handful,
that shine in the small change of life.
They are balm to the soul that is woeful,
and loyal right up to the Grim Reaper's scythe,
they sustain your right to be hopeful.
True friends are gold, by the handful,
that shines in the small change of life.

R J Gould

A Time Honoured

Young then; no wistful spirit
yet disturbed our conscience;
no doubts rebarbed sorrows reminisced
nor yet curbed or cursed our curiosity.

We didn't wonder who we were
or yet know that worst of broken promises.
The death of youth;
the sharpest spoil of life's untruth.

So, sure of our immortality we played and loved,
embracing all, fearing none,
and passing time on nought of substance,
we passed our lives in living,
not in fearing that they'd soon be gone.

Peering back from longer teeth,
there's no sorrow for the way we lived,
but only now a sound belief
that we were right in living life the way we did,
to be just us; without pretence; without ado;
for time tells us one thing that's surely true;
we none of us can raise a smile
remembering what we didn't do.

Jim Rogerson

Claudia

We met as children, in a coffee-shop.
She wore a hat and gloves while I
Was casual in my nonchalance
Surrounded by my friends.
But something in her stance attracted me
And step by lingering step we walked
Into our life long amity.
School days were spent together, and our leisure.
I was the leader then, the flirt,
While she was shy; but all that changed.
War came, she joined the ATS and went away.
She then took on a different personality.
Yet through the years we kept in touch
With postcards from abroad, long distance calls,
And always when we met, things were as yesterday.
No need for explanation or a long discourse.
The years went by, and in my mind,
She was forever young, but then she died.
I miss her still.

Christina Stowell

Farewell To Gerry

Today my heart is heavy
In fact I am rather sad
I had to go and say farewell
To my (second dad)
Although I have cried a million tears
I am glad I knew him all those years
He has left behind his family
All who loved him so
But when our time is finally up
I am afraid we have to go
We just cannot linger in the past
Life is for the living, however long it lasts

T Marriott

GrandFriends

(For Daryl, Emily, Chloe, Kerrie and Linsey)

One Tuesday lunch time just ten years ago
I had a special visit from Adrian and Jo,
The six months passed so quickly then Daryl came along,
His Dad was so excited that he burst out into song!
A trophy gained for football, and a leader in the cubs
He beats the Drum at Church Parade, but still has time for hugs!

When Stuart and Julie visited next they were grinning from ear to
ear,
And gave us the news at last we had all been waiting to hear
Excitement came on Wednesday, while we waited by the phone
It rang at 6pm, our granddaughter was born.
Emily came with jet black hair and little rosebud lips
At eight years old her hair's now blond, and has a fashionable swing
of the hips
So proud are we to watch her dance and swim
At Brownies she's a star as she keeps her team in trim!

Chloe came the next year in the winter time so cold
We had the call on Saturday night too come quite quick were told!
She is our Xmas baby with lots of long black hair
Who very soon was smiling and dribbling without a care
She did not crawl just bounced along never to be left behind
At seven she reads, writes and paints everything she can find.

Kerrie and Linsey came together, a little before their due
Two sisters for Daryl, with deep red hair and sparkling eyes of blue
Kerrie who's logic puts the world to right
While Linsey loves to chat even through the night!
Granddad's the target for games and lots of fun
Whilst we all admire their Trophy for ballet well done!

They all call me Nanny Bubble because Beryl was to hard.
And I love it . . .
Nanny Bubble . . .

Beryl Davis

A Tribute To Andrew Mundy

(To Andy, from all his friends at the Cotswold gravel pits)

Flickering shadows in the water,
Upon time's fleeting wings,
Robs angling of its talent,
And the warmth, that friendship brings.

Always 'tis the brightest star,
A lifetime far too short,
Though achievements and the memories,
Death can ne'er abort.

The Andy that we knew, is gone,
Yet in spirit ever there,
With each ripple on the shoreline,
Scattering shafts of sunlight fair.

As the curtained rain sweeps softly,
From an ever-darkening sky,
Farewell friend - we'll not forget,
For we cannot reason why.

John Nolan

From This World

From this world
Now he has gone
While with us
A light he shone

Like a beacon
In the dark
And on us
He left a mark

Now way up yonder
In the sky
Where people go
When people die

That holy land
We must all share
Where angels watch
And saints take care

My father now
Has passed away
And up there
He's gone to stay

He passed away
While in his sleep
And the Lord
Now him will keep

Lex Coghill

My Friend

Henry, I've owned many a year
Comforted me, when I'd shed a tear
Couldn't sleep, if not in my bed
Prayed for him, when prayers were said
Never without him for a single day
Whether at work, or at play,
When growing up, having to work.
He went with me, though I felt a jerk!
I really loved, my dear old friend
Not to my own child, could I lend.
Is worn with age, afraid to say
Looks so sad, when words do flay.
Never to be parted through thick or thin
To throw him out, would be a sin,
Old and tattered, even threadbare
Is one eyed Henry, my teddy bear.

I K Skinner

Memory

Alone in my bed I lie,
A lie,
Closer to the truth,
For in my mind, you lie,
For in my arms you stay -
So close,
At what cost memory,
Your kiss -
Your touch -
Your smell -
Your - , now a dream yet,
In sleep remain -
To dream -

P G Beaugeard

The Ventnor Pedalos

Remember the days on the Isle of Wight,
When we walked over soft sands,
Revelling in our childhood delight,
As we approached brand new lands,
Those are the days that I'll never forget,
Some memories can never be lost.

Secrets we have shared and kept,
Always will we hold their treasure,
Though often we have wept,
For each others lack of pleasure,
These are the things that come with best friends,
Upon our side compassion lends.

I could never find a friend as true,
Someone to talk when I'm sad and blue.
Whatever may happen in years to come,
You'll always be my special chum!

Tracey Ann Heard

An Ode To My Friends

From out of the darkness -
You came, like a glimmer of light
You gave my life new meaning
Along with hope and insight
You showed me the way to happiness
And you taught me how to be
Tougher and much stronger
And to fight heroically
I used to feel so lonely
No friends to care for me
But then my prayers were answered
Like a miracle, you came to me
You embraced me with your kindness
Your humour and your love
You're so caring and considerate
Were you sent from up above?
O you truly are someone
I never wish to lose
And I want you to know
As a friend, I love you

Wendy Ripsher

The Joy Of Your Smile

Like the song of a bird,
like the notes of a chorus,
like music in spring
is the joy of your smile.

Like the softness of silk,
like the touch of a hand,
like the magic of spring
is the joy of your smile.

Like a taste which is subtle,
like the blending of spices,
like the flavour of springtime
is the joy of your smile.

Like the scent of the forest,
like the fragrance of flowers,
like the freshness of spring
is the joy of your smile.

Like the beam of a lighthouse,
like the peace of a rainbow,
like the colours of springtime
is the joy of your smile.

Suzanne Low Steenson

Barbara Ann

Barbara Ann The Beach Boys sang,
And bells of remembrance in my head rang.
A beautiful little girl, with long, blonde hair,
My mind goes back and I feel I'm there.
It is the sixties and you are my friend,
Ages ten and thirteen, our personalities blend.
You enjoy The Avengers, Mrs Peel and Steed,
We watch the TV and lots of books we read.
Your Uncle Michael is your favourite guy,
We're his biggest fans, you and I.
He films you on camera prancing about,
You sing and you dance, and scream and shout.
We used to make plans when you'd come to my school,
Sometimes you'd be nervous, but I'd say it's cool.
I came home from school, I had no idea,
There were no signs, you had no fear.
My mum explained you'd died in your sleep,
You didn't feel nothing as the Angels did creep.
They took you to Heaven to be a film star,
And I know you'll be happy wherever you are.
It's a long time ago, but I'll never forget you.
I'm so glad we were friends and I'm happy I met you.

Denise Clitheroe

Remembering Friends

It's a tradition - not a modern trend
To call and see a dear old friend.
Friendship that has remained unbroken
From those times - and very rarely spoken.

We'll greet each other with respect,
Circumstances, or attire we don't inspect.
Encounters together in the past
Were rough and we were always last!

This is not the time to be forlorn
We count ourselves - newly born.
We survived - that's no mistake.
Our hands will clasp - no need to shake.

Is there a future waiting there for us?
We've been, and seen, without a fuss
We both understand with clarity
That sounding brass, is not charity.

We can no longer stand or march,
With legs as stiff as if of starch,
When silence falls - we're in the park
Marching to 'The Rising of the Lark'.

Frank Williams

Michael - My Brother

I received some sad news, just the other day.
That my long lost brother, had sadly passed away.
The sadness I felt, how could I ever explain.
Many lost years, now I carry a brother's pain.

Our youthful years, gone forever, spent apart.
Memories of him, were hidden in my heart.
It has saddened me greatly, knowing he has gone.
Together in Heaven, with mum and dad, a loving son.

All those years apart, in another country he lived.
The joys of friendship to each other, we could have give
A friend, a brother, now he is in heaven up above.
At peace with mum and dad, giving him their love.

Many words could have been said, but now it's too late.
He'll be welcome in heaven, through shiny golden gates.
A prayer I will say, for my brother each night.
A new star in heaven, shining down his light.

Many years have passed us by, they are lost, now gone.
His memory will be with me, 'till the end of a dying sun.
Michael - my brother, why did this happen, this way.
You will live in my heart, a prayer each night I will say.

Kevin P Collins

The Apparition

We wondered day long, he and I,
Through a landscape golden with the
Onset of autumn,
Meandering through mire and fen,
Subdued by the sublime majesty of the land:
The days companions, fellow travellers of the
Light; engrossed in the sorcerer's unfolding
Charms; disobeying his bidding at the stile
To turn back and begone.
Onward we pressed, stumbling over the tussocks,
Mindful of our trespass; gaining the rise,
And a parting glimpse of the purple gown.

Stealthily now, and in haste. But what's amiss?
What terror assails without reason?
We, rooted to the spot, and trembling?

Then it appeared: a white luminescence
Faintly transparent, drifting across the path,
And as quickly vanished!

Tentatively we searched, hearts pounding;
Emboldened, the presence gone, with braver probings,
Aught was found.

Was it shadow? Or substance?
A trick of fading light?

The curlews warbled to the counterpoint of
The herring gull's cry;
Lost in the inscrutable marshes:
Their fiery pools emblazoned
With an enigmatic smile.

Malcolm G Cooper

For Joyce, November 1998
(With permission from David, her husband, our friend)

It was a long time -
Three decades.
Across speeding years
Our friendship grew,
A real possession
On the changing tides
Of Life.
The sunlit hills
Smiled kindly
On our little joys,
Those trivia,
Building blocks
Of happiness.

Now the fogs
Of sadness
Circle all about,
The heart is leaden,
And tears prick
The eyes.
But hidden love
Outlasts
This great divide,
Ageless, eternal.

Roger M Creegan

Janet

We met when I was seven, you were nine.
Hours we played in the summer sunshine.
Took carefree rides on the old oak tree's bough.
So many bright days I remember now,
Cinema trips, cycling and birthday tea.
To Grammar School you went ahead of me.
Still we met and talked of our hopes and dreams.
Much has happened, long ago that time seems.
You went away as a teacher to train.
We wrote letters until we met again.
Through the years you taught many miles away,
Then you called with something special to say.
You were engaged, your bridesmaid would be me.
Your wedding is a happy memory.
Then, your son was born and your dreams came true.
As Godmother, I shared your joy with you.
Through the years there was always our friendship.
For my wedding, you made a special trip.
Then, came pain and months of adversity
But always shone through your serenity.
The last sad day, when I sat by your side,
'Do not go, my friend,' silently I cried.
I remember you now with thankfulness
And the dear friendship that my life did bless.
As I wander along Memory's lane:
You are riding the oak tree's bough again.
I know that for you, new life has begun.
In our hearts you are loved, forever young.

Margaret Williams

Precious Gift

With precious thoughts I reminisce
About my friend of many years.
Every time I think of her
My heart just moves and stirs.
Fate was more than gracious
When we moved to live next door.
I just could not imagine
Just what there was in store.

We enjoyed each other's company
Our families got on great,
Such fun, laughter, happiness, this was surely fate
There was love and care, we would share
These years were really something rare.
Then our lives changed
We had to suddenly move away,
My friend and family also could not stay.

Now between us was an ocean
We were now miles apart.
Letters fluttered through the door
As our dog would pick them off the floor.
The telephone account was really bad
To chat helped us not to feel so sad.

Now the parting of the way has past
These precious years went by too fast.
Our friendship will remain precious and true
The memories remain ever new.
It was a privilege to have and hold
Far more precious than silver or gold.
Until in time we meet again
Thing will never be the same.

Aves Swanson

Time To Regret

'He quite often talked about you,'
she said between sobs
as we walked through the drizzle
between wet gravestones.
In a moment of silence
I wondered who had lied,
for he had never been friendly
and argued most of the time.
He always looked elsewhere
as if you were boring
and would quickly rush off
if he saw someone important.
And yet, and yet often
we laughed together
which leaves me puzzling
in this chill weather.

J Sharratt

True Friendship

Darkness.
The dark night of depression.
No ray of light to pierce the overpowering gloom.
Even faith,
That faith that once was strong and true,
Has gone.
Nothing.
The will to live sapped and withered.

Into that darkness,
Into that void,
He came.
A firm true friend,
Willing that life should go on,
A rock to cling to in a sea of despair.
There.
There.
Never letting go.
Steadfast.
'I'll always be there!'

Roma Davies

Remembering Friends

And when November came we changed the garden,
Rebuilt the summer-room, re-laid the lawn
More as a tribute to your memory
Than of necessity since you have gone.

You would have loved the many subtle changes
Made to the rose arbour, the laurel lane
In such a fervour of activity
As if we thought you might return again.

Somewhere is a grave, austere, unprotected
Beneath a foreign sky we have not seen,
But part of you stays in this English garden,
Safe now and like the Yew tree evergreen.

Leaves of the oak in richly toned mutations
Lie on the grass, a chill is on the air,
Winter will come, but now is autumn's glory
Which holds your essence and we find you there.

Frances M Searle

Nature's Child

The Gods bemoan, your sad demise,
Those sounds you hear, are cherub's sighs,
That moisture glistening, is not dew,
Those weeping flowers, shed tears for you,
The birds are stilled, they sing no song,
For you, they mourn, for you, they long,
For truly were you, 'nature's child',
Akin, with all that's good and mild,
You danced thro' life, like Zephyr's breeze
Your one desire, was just to please,
That, this, you did, was plain to see
At one with nature, most perfectly.

Francis W T Cooper

Tears Sparkle Like Pearls

Jewels sparkle like a pearl
Splashing softly to the floor
A cascading waterfall
They are tightly closed
But still they seep
Escape and run free

Angela Couzens

I Know Because I Am That Man

I remember Arthur saying 'If I was thirty years younger we would
have made a top team'.

When I was a boy Arthur taught me to box and now I box clever,
when I was at school he wished I'd get a good education - so I went
to college.
When I was at college he said I should be working but England was
gripped by the second Eighties recession and riots loomed.

I scrapped through and he survived, as he went into decline I went
from strength to strength and joined the corporation, the Council
went bust and the corporation disbanded.

I found solitude in Arthur and our weekly Sunday outings, sometimes
a bind, othertimes the most memorable experience and foresight into
history past and present.

Vesting day was followed by Next Steps and then Leaps.
Time had took its toll, Arthur hung on refusing to give up the
ghost/but on whose behalf.

He was half gone and I was way there.
A career had developed into an occupation and an occupation into a
dream come true.

Then it hits you - those closest also go their own way, Arthur slipped
away while I was busy making hay.

Those that knew him missed him as much as me.
Now he's scattered across the ground no longer to be found.
I now walk the path in his footsteps . . . so who am I?
Great family, great friend, if thirty years younger then probably my
best man . . . but then there-be no me.

Simon James Walker

No Strings Attached

Perhaps an ambition of all of us is to be loved in someway by
   everyone.
We know it makes the world go round and it's what soaps and
   films rely on.
However, the meaning of love has been interpreted in many
   different ways.
There are some who respect this, but the romantic element has
   altered since the early days.
It should be the culmination of a friendship where two become
   almost as one.
And with a lifetime of closeness have enjoyed every year that's come
   and gone.
There are those less fortunate and unable to fulfil such a dream.
But love to them is still an essential, although there's no partner
   in the scheme.
Here the love that can be exchanged with friends, needs extra special
   care.
It does not call for commitment or obligation - it's so very rare.
So although those on their own occasionally feel a close relationship
   would be ideal.
There is love and friendship from so many that we know we can rely
   on - and that is very real.

Reg Morris

Welcome Visitor

Aunty Nellie's here again
See her through the windowpane
Creeping and peeping she does appear
Her Annual visit to us each year.
Dressed in white and brightest green
'Lily of the Valley'
Whose perfume's supreme.
Many, many years ago
There was two young girls
A special friendship grew
And shared together through the years
Happiness, secrets, sometimes tears.
During their lifetime of giving and caring
Garden plants were exchanged
Gifts they delighted in sharing
So that is how it came to be
'Lily of the Valley'
From Aunty Nellie's garden
To my Mothers, then to me
Now, as each springtime comes around
With joy, this plant bursts from the ground
Gazing out during April showers
There's Aunty Nellie smiling
Through those delicate flowers.

Sheila Margaret Parker

She's OK!
(Dedicated to Sylvia, a true friend)

She's high, she's low,
she's fast, she's slow.

Suppressed, possessed?

No, manic depressed.

She's sad, she's mad,
she's bad, she's glad.

Regressed, distressed?

No, manic depressed.

Her mania is zanier
than your average depression,
a challenge for any
in a therapy profession.
But come what may,
this lady's OK,
a success
who is manic depressed.

Alexander K Stubbs

Alone

I watch the smoke
Drifting aimlessly
In grey directionless trendils.
As I lie on my bed
And think.
I watch the window.
Standing motionless,
Trapped, as I am,
Within these walls.

As my thoughts reach
Their stale brink
I watch my tired image
Of imaginary you.
Thinking all kinds of
Left behind things.
Fluid was the memory
From which I drank
And of all the things
I seem to do
There's always the
Memory of you.

Sonya B

Margaret My Soul Mate

When it's part of yourself you're describing
It's hard to know where to begin
It's not something immediately visible
It comes naturely from deep within
We really are just like a puzzle
Dysfunctional parts at His feet
Then He puts us together - pieces fit
And then the picture's complete.
We are often taken for sisters
We always deny it of course
Our father however knows better
And put you where you are needed most.
Through all of our bad times you've been there
We've had some good times too.
Though lately's been so very hard it's difficult to see
How without you we'd have pulled through
So thankyou for being my soul-mate
Thankyou for just being you
My spare-part, someone to depend on
Loyal, supportive, and always true.

Barbara Symons

The Brave Ones

In days of old
When men were bold
And they went off to war,
We were spared and were not told,
Of the horrors that they saw,
We stayed at home, we prayed for them,
And of course, we wished them well,
We are proud of those men, today and then,
For they have so much to tell.

Ena Andrews

Memory Of Love

Across the village sorrowed and mourned
A new day begins, sky-sunrise adorned
Like our Lord Jesus Mum's death's not in vain
With undying love she has risen again.

Up on the hilltop there's a special place
Looking across to the sea for another face;
So let us take a stroll - will you walk with me?
I'm in love with my Mother's Memory.

Amidst the trees, flowers and birds
Every footstep echo my Mother's words
Love, Feel, Touch and See;
I'm in love with my Mother's Memory.

Roses heavenly scented look up to the skies
Gently swaying to flitting butterflies
Their wings of gossamer so delicately born
Like woven threads on Mother's shroud adorn
A walk of love, beauty and grace
Mum is here in this exceptional place;
A Memory of devotion this worthy place will be
Son and Daughter are in love with their Mum's Memory.

Every step along this special place;
Reflects the warmth of our Mother's face
Her perfume, smile and endless care
Echoed by the rustling trees in scented air.

On that last fateful day
They took not our Mother away
My Father kissed away her pain;
Hand - Hand they walk together again;
In this special place - Look, Listen you'll see
Dearest Brother - be happy Mum, Pop together are free.

Ann Marie

Doreen's Dream

One night she had a dream
It brought back memories past
Gone my empty days without purpose
She changed my life, at last

'In my dream you were reciting poems about Blackpool
Though when I do not know'
We decided it was in our school days
More than fifty years ago

My friend Doreen was a busy lady
Used to run our sequence dance
Organise our seaside holidays
Always planning, nothing left to chance

'You are our own Pam Eyres' she said
It made me feel quite grand
'Will you read your poems on our next holiday
An Old Time Music Hall I've planned'

I started to write my poems again
After years of resting my pen
Filling an empty retirement alone
With a purpose in life lacking until then

I sent off a poem to a magazine
To see my first poem in print, what a thrill
The pleasure my hobby gives me
An ambition I've been able to fulfil

Now my work is in many anthologies
My friend, gone to the dance in the sky
But I shall never forget her encouragement
And the dream she had, 'till I die.

Peggy Hunter

A Friend

When you're in trouble and at your wits end,
Then is the time when you so need a friend.
One to whom you can confide.
To all of those troubles, that are on your mind.

Those innermost, hopeless, forlorn despairs,
Are so greatly lessened, when somebody cares.
Then when hidden thoughts, you can unfold
And when at last, your stories told.

You will find from silent, inward grief,
You will have gained, such a great relief.
All because you had that good, kind friend.
Who listened to your tale until the end.

No greater comfort can you get.
Than that from a friend, who cares in depth!
My old friend, so very dear.
Passed on, yet in my heart.
                    Still near.

William Holmes

Gone

Gone is that smile that struggled through the pain
Those grey-blue eyes I'll never see again
Gone is that voice, though I can hear it still
If I am blessed perhaps I always will.

Gone too is all the music that she made
That she composed, conducted, sang and played
Her sewing box lies idle on the chair
Her artist paints and brushes too are there.

And in the garden ripening in the sun
Plump strawberries - we picked some once for fun
And sat and ate them there beneath the tree
One simple pleasure that she shared with me.

And everywhere, in wild profusion, flowers
She planted in her last leisure hours
I see her working there on hands and knees
Her fair hair ruffled by the fragrant breeze.

From every plant, from every bush and tree
Memories of yesterday creep hauntingly.
Though she is gone, fond memories will remain
Until that day, please God, we meet again.

Estelle James

Friends

Here I am a friend indeed
met some nice people we both agreed
these friends of ours are Dave and Lynn
we opened our hearts and let them in,
these friends of our shared our lives
the husbands got on and on so did the wives.
A perfect combination in these troubled times
with the theft and muggings and other crimes.
We have a laugh and call each other
it's all good fun like sister and brother
we'd shared our lives and was content
we'd shared our dreams if not invent.
We've been on holiday for a week or two
there wasn't alot we didn't do
the men played snooker which was quite funny
the women played bingo to try and win back money
we didn't win much but it was fun.
We stayed indoors there wasn't much sun.
In the years gone by we'd visit weekends
not because we had too, because we are friends.

James E Royle

To A Very Old Lady

She climbs the last few uphill steps to Heaven
Bent double: still her love and patience shine
Enchanting all, who, loving, feel her leaven
Make their hearts rise. Oh wearisome incline!
Her body tires, taking its toll in pains
In closed horizons: such a tiny round
Encompasses her. But she comfort gains
From all her family. The welcome sounds,
Voices beloved, that reassure her days
Transform her. All her gentle soul
Lives in her smile. And now a trenchant phrase
Bubbles up laughter, keeps our spirits whole.
Life lived in love and giving - what's to learn?
Nothing. But all to teach us, in our turn.

Frances Searle

Victor, My Very Best Friend

They say that Time is always here.
Somehow I know it's true.
For in my heart, I still can feel

The love I have for you.

I close my eyes and I can see
A scene from long ago,
A time when you were here with me.

You loved me, too, I know.

So many scenes, it's like a book
I'm taking from a shelf.
Those happy days and loving nights
I'm showing to myself.

I cannot hear you speaking now,

But I can see the place.
And I imagine I can feel
Your hand upon my face,

A gentle touch, a prelude to our kissing,
A thousand times a day I know, it's you that I am missing.

Kathleen Abbott

Feathered Friend

Feathered friend in the garden
Picking berries of scarlet red
Sang and chirped the sweetest song
That I had ever heard
I looked to see from whence it came
There amongst the leaves of gold and jade.

A song bird full of praise and glee
Sang a refrain whilst flapping
Hopping dancing dramatically.
'Was that thrush saying thanks
For the crumbs on the tray?'
Or to welcome a visitor.

To the garden that crisp autumn day
Ah, no, I don't think it was any of these
Thrush was happy in the garden
Giving thanks to God for fresh fruit on the trees.
Faithful song bird warbling thrush.
Have I captured a friend, feathered friend I can trust.

Psalm 145V18
The Lord is nigh unto all them that call upon him,
to all that call upon him in truth.

Frances Gibson

My Friend

My friend was someone I turned to when no-one else seemed to
care;
When I needed a shoulder to cry on I knew she'd always be there;
She listened to all of my problems with a patience beyond all belief,
Just quietly hearing my troubles, willing to share all my grief.
She didn't lay blame on my doorstep, she just helped me to see a way
through,
With a smile and a hug she just whispered, 'I know, luv, for I've
been there, too.'
After talking things over together, I felt I had lightened my load,
For I'd shared with another my worries, someone who'd been down
the same road.
The future then seemed so much brighter, I felt I was able to cope,
Thanks to my friend who had listened and taught me the meaning of
hope.

Kathleen Poulton

Souvenirs

Mementoes, souvenirs,
Call them what you will,
I have them all,
Here with me still,
Those pressed flowers from the bouquet,
You brought me that frosty December,
Such a beautiful array of colour
Do you still remember?
That empty champagne bottle,
Left from our summer celebration,
Now with a candle atop,
Making a special decoration,
That little black dress,
I wore when we first met,
I've never parted with it,
Oh no, not as yet,
All those lovely cards,
From Christmas and Valentine days,
I still have them all,
Neatly stored away,
Every single item,
Shares a memory with me,
Of you and the good times,
And how great life can be.

Anne Williams

My Friend Mary

A lady of quality,
That's what you are.
Helping out others,
Both near and far.

An elegant lady,
With plenty of flair.
Helping out others,
Showing you care.

Those who have known you,
Think you have style.
Qualities within you,
Make people smile.

A lady of quality.
What is your worth!
To all who have known you.
You're the Salt of this Earth.

M Ridgway

My Regret

I am filled with nostalgia and also remorse
I've heard that an old neighbour has finished life's course
A neighbour who was a big part of my past
It's a very long time since I saw her last

Nostalgia is in remembering the good days gone by
Remorse is the sadness, I hadn't said goodbye
I had promised to visit old neighbours of mine
But each opportunity that came I'd decline
Thinking, I will go to see them some other day
Forgetting that time passes too quickly away

Time really goes by at a terrific rate
Now that I have some, I've left it too late
To say cheerio to that nice old friend
Whose days I didn't know had come to an end

There are not many left from my days as a boy
So I must resolve that I won't be so coy
When I hear of another old friend, or more
I will definitely go and knock on their door

Hal Takata

Beloved

I remember you in moonlight
Crisp cold winter nights,
Our muffled breaths
Twin trails of wraithlike mist.

I remember you in sunlight
The scent of moss crushed underfoot,
The lark's song sweet
Above the fragrant heather.

I remember you in rain
Picking drenched raspberries,
Hair dripping wet,
Hands cold and berry stained.

But most of all I remember you
By the fire on a quiet evening.
Eyes half closed in relaxation,
The comfort of your silent presence.

Elizabeth Gwilliam

My Uncle Hugo

(Dedicated to Hugo Rosato who died on 12th May 1996 at the Royal Marsden Hospital. London)

As Lord Denning's Chauffeur
  He called you 'my man',
And forever that phrase, will be in our clan.
  Your spirit and tact, was SAS trained,
Not to eat rats or rodents,
  But from Aden, you named.
Your family of five, with three wives
  Passed with you,
And all of us knew you as 'Hue'.
When in West Oxfordshire the Council,
  They took your life free;
The destruction of Southcombe,
  Adversely the deed was undone upon thee.
Then the cancer, it killed you,
  And ate hard at your soul.
My truly beloved uncle,
  I've fought for the Roll.
To right all those wrongs,
  In trust to your name.
As Rosato, not Ross,
Whilst the masons have fallen,
  And are buried in blame.
Your spirit, your courage,
  And your heart, for us all.
You're never forgotten,
  Even after God made his call.
Your mother Rosina, and your brother John,
  Still keep the Magnolia,
With your story still told.
  Always my uncle, and loved so dear,
You've showed me to life, and life without fear.

Anthony Rosato

The Church Bursar

He didn't carry a cross
Of rough hewn wood,
But a burden of accounting,
A weight of ledgers and journals,
A balancing act of facts and figures,
Right down to the last, rebellious penny.

His back was not scarred,
Nor his palms pierced through.
But bent by years of bending,
Bending over and conforming
To a desk, and the rules of the game.
Hands worn smooth by paper and pen.

Beneath this financial carefulness,
A careful spirit was there
Serving the servants of God,
Clearing the mounting rubble of detail,
So church and people could walk
Freely, unhindered on their way.

How many? So many
Have been enriched by his generous,
Untrumpeted giving.
The marks of his faithfulness and loyalty
Will survive both here and there.
For, 'They take with them a record of their deeds.'*

*Revelation Ch 14 v 13

Gordon Harper

Mary

Mary, dear friend of my childhood days,
Wiser than me in so many ways,
Cheerful and caring, loyal and true,
Our friendship was stable all her life through.
The canal at Devizes was our swimming pool,
Where diving off locks was against the rule -
But the young see no fear when danger is nigh,
And we opened lock gates when the barges went by.
While blackberry picking one day in the sun
We were chased by a bull, which wasn't much fun!
The farmer was cross, we'd no right to be there,
But we'd ignored the sign which told us 'Beware'.
Hopscotch on the pavement, the squares all chalked out,
Scrumping the apples in fields round about.
Roller skates, marbles, spinning tops too,
Pleasures were simple, ambitions were few.
Walks to 'Olivers' camp' and picnics galore
All came to an end with the advent of war.
Our paths separated, our childhood was done,
Carefree days were behind us, 'til victory was won.
Life at times had been tough, but the letters we sent
Kept us in contact wherever we went.
The years went by swiftly, and then came the day
When illness claimed Mary, and took her away.
I've never forgotten the days of our youth,
And now that I've got 'A bit old in the tooth'
I think of her often, with affection always,
Mary, dear friend of my childhood days.

Catherine R Gamble

Gone Too Soon

Why did you go?
Why did you join the march
Away from me - away from life
On into eternal paths.

Into pastures new you passed
Unknown to me and still unknown
When you have changed from life to Life
How will I know you so?

I will know you by the love reaching back
To gather me in the way
That will lead me on to where you march
Ever on - oh, why did you not stay.

Mary Gilbert

My Friend, My Father

I think of my father a lot, kind he was, but strict.
We went for walks and he knew a lot about
animals, birds and Rabbie Burns.
He'd find a nest among the ferns
and up the burn he could tickle trout
or uncover a ball of baby mice under a hayrick.
He took me with him to football games
teaching respect for sport and skill;
Good save! Good shot! Well done!
Even when the other side won
he said that generosity, truth and honour will
fulfil your life in all its frames.
He told me stories of Scotland's past,
Of Wallace and Bruce and others
and he made me proud and glad.
He knew a lot did my Dad,
he told to me, and my brothers,
things that our lifetime will last.
How much of me is him
I really do not know
but Crawford, me and Jim
What we are, to him we owe.

David B Welsh

118

Valley Lads Of Childhood

The dingle dales of hills and vales
Bore footsteps childhood dance.
The young time burnt and all the flame,
Ran to the fire of youthful chance.
Down the meadowland of tortuous trail,
Where the robbers hid in delay,
Beside the brook where the dead sheep took,
No note of youth's gateway.
What ease of heart did friendship make,
In the days of no limit time.
Where pigskin flight and honed willow bats,
Joyed with swallow and celendine.
Spewed up from down earth's heart of black,
Mini mountains of our fathers' travail,
Rose in abandon within that habitat,
To a freedom where once was a jail.
In cellulose epic we the rivers dammed,
For youth's aura was much silver screen.
And never was ever a contemplate,
There be shallow waters to our dream.
This was our childhood of embraced content,
For each day a grandiose scheme.
We heroed the battles for all of the world,
Though home, was just Mum o'er the green.
Then seeming sudden our morning was done,
Another chapter did the hours unfurl.
No more so important this saving the world,
Not half as important, as a girl.

Elwyn Johnson

Some Eternal Sun

Our lives have altered now, my love
But still I feel quite sure
The rising sun as seen by me
Lights your world even more.

The beauty that is here on earth
Trees, flowers, fields and skies
That fills my heart with joy must be
More vibrant to your eyes.

For you have wider knowledge now
Than my earth-shackled soul
You'll see all life for what it is
And know the final goal.

But we shall meet again, my love
When my life here is done
We'll rendezvous outside this earth
'Neath some eternal sun.

Stephanie Reiersen

Through You
(Win - Salvation Army Wetherby, Yorkshire)

I stood alone
You looked across
A smile upon your face
You took my hand, a loving embrace
A thing I never had.

You may not know God's plan for you
You just practice what he says
And as I've learned about your God.
I find I'm rich in friends
I look across see your smile
I know I'm not alone.

I thank the Lord for showing me
The riches he has in store.
For through your smile
Your warm embrace
The twinkle of your eyes
I feel the comfort and power of God.
      I know I'm not alone.

Susan Bell

Ex-Ray

My smoke,
drifting
into darkness,
reminds me of
her milky bones
in the X-ray,
and how we
watched her disappear,
like a puff of smoke,
and leave the fire
burning in our hearts.

Stewart Cardno

Daddy's Little Girl

A little girl, a loving Dad,
the bestest friend she ever had,
he made her laugh, he made her cry,
why did you go and leave her, die?

An older girl with coloured hair,
her Dad was hard at times, always fair,
with her weird clothes and music too,
dear Dad, she thought the world of you.

That same little girl, she stands alone,
her Daddy's gone, he won't be home,
her heart is broke, her eyes are red,
a kiss goodnight Dad, she climbs into bed.

Wendy Bage

Ode To Jo

Jo was a friend in the very best sense
To all those who knew her - the list is immense
Although in the throes of a dreaded disease
Her main aim in life was to care and to please.
On greeting she always would ask after you
Your wife, child or husband or others she knew
On leaving, she always admonished, 'Take care,
Of your dear little self, and God bless you, my dear'
Always turning your queries away from herself
Except telling stories she reached from the shelf
Of her memories and times past in Bury St Ed,
And the Baker's shop kept by her folks, long since dead
They may be gone but her stories stayed true
And raised fun and laughter to all she told to.
Her memory for detail was very acute
Though we did sometimes wonder? Such lines she would shoot
Her home would resound with the laughter she raised
As she acted out parts of the folk she portrayed.
Who could describe this friend so unique
It would take many books, for she had a technique
Only possessed by so very few
She was loved by the masses, because she loved you.
Yes! You - You and You, she missed no one out
Her lungs they were faulty but her heart was real stout
She had time for Everyone, Young, Old, Big or Small
If you needed a friend she was always 'On Call'.
She deserved 'Rest and Peace' but I fear that she'll wait
'Til she's checked with St Peter that he's really 'Alraight!'
She'll chat up the angels and then will rejoice
That she's breathless no longer and can still use her voice
As she tells them the news of the life now removed

From her friends here below where she lived, laughed and loved.
She'll not be forgotten for many long years
By the friends left behind - and there's bound to be tears
But thinking of you, Jo - we can't help but think
Of your sweet roguish smile and your wicked old wink!

Elizabeth White

A Star Named Laura

You asked if I could write a poem, just for you,
I pondered as to which words can best describe you.
I needed inspiration from the heavens above,
the words came to me via a messenger's dove.

I looked up to that great expanse of
darkened sky, something extraordinarily
bright caught my eye.
It was a glistening star, sparkling
much brighter than the rest,
of all the stars in the universe
it stood out for all to see,
so distinctive unique they say.

Of all the stars in the universe,
a star so bright could not
remain without a name.
So I named it Laura after you,
as you have such sparkling eyes,
and are everso bright, clever,
helpful, considerate too, and
that's all I have to say about you.

So Laura if you would like to see
your reflection in the dead of night,
just look to that star shining
so bright.

Jeff Reay

True Blue

She seems to know how I feel
this friend of mine.
She's there for me
at any old time.
I yell, shout, and sometimes scream,
but she stands her ground
looking quite serene.
Then she looks at me
so knowing and wise,
the love shining through
those big golden eyes.
I know this friend
will always remain true.
'Who is she?' You ask,
it's my cat 'Muffin'
A British Blue.

Kelly Mitchell

Robyn

When I was saying my prayers last night
I asked my God to shed some light . . .
I asked my God to tell my why
did little Robyn never fly?

I said 'Dear God she could have been
a doctor, a lawyer - a beauty queen,'
but with infinite wisdom came this reply
'My child - yours is not to reason why.'

'You say little Robyn never flew
alas - my child that's just not true,'
'In the arms of Jesus she came to me
I gave her wings and set her free.'

Scot Crone

Mind's Eye

I sit in my chair, remembering with a sigh
And images rise floating into my mind's eye.
Then the question comes to me
How can I see
Something that has been sinking and drowning
In those hidden recesses
That can only be brought to the surface again
With whispers and caresses?
But I suppose I won't know that until I die,
And meet again my friend and laugh instead of cry,
For she'll be waiting at those gates for me
And once again her dear sweet face I'll see.

Paddy Jupp

Andrew

Nine lives, at least,
And in the brief time that I knew you,
I guess you used them all.
I used to think it was a lack of imagination
That made you so fearless,
But that wasn't true;
More a lack of percipience
When it came to those little things called
Consequences.
Me:
I was far too smart for my own daring,
And as we tore down impossible gradients
On our Heath Robinson bogies,
I could already see the blood and hair on the tarmac.
You could have seen it, too,
But for you,
The thrill of the chase overrode the brake of reason,
And it simply never occurred to you to look.

But then,
I guess the world needs fearless people like you,
People whose actions aren't hampered by heed,
Who do first and relish or regret later;
People who live for the moment
And die by the second.
Without them,
How would people like me grow old?

John Kirkbride

A Very Dear Friend

My friend of many years Mollie
Will always be most dear
She is so jolly and full of kindness
One can rely on her at all times
Mollie will bend over backwards
To help me when in great need
Sparks of gladness beam within me
When I see her walking down my road
She seems to give out an astounding glow
And will welcome me always
With a jolly, 'Hello'
What a treasure to know
She would never leave me to wayward go
Advice from Mollie one can be sure
Always benefits me and if in awe
Turn huge mountain thoughts into tiny
                                mole hills
We many a day laugh and joke concerning
                        our everlasting bills
No doubt life would be extremely dull
Without Mollie and her satisfying
                        sweetened mull!

Alma Montgomery Frank

Daniela

By phone I was told with your mother in tears,
my heart skipped a beat as I placed the receiver.
My head began spinning at the thought of the news,
so sickened I cried like a child.

We were due to meet up, talk on old times, go out,
then so suddenly you were taken away.
Your death really hit me,
the hurt still lives with me,
I never had chance to tell you goodbye.

        Goodbye Daniela
        God Bless

Samantha Jayne Rees

Doctor Preston

Doctor Preston was his name,
a wonderful doctor,
he felt our pain.
Time will pass, but.
Pain will not end.
Life carries on,
our memory will not end.
Captured in our hearts and soul.
Always with us never growing old.
God bless.

Marion Lee

My Old Friend

Somehow, he has been here through thick and thin,
Helped me with ideas that I believe in.
And he has been my friend for many years,
Sharing always my laughter and my tears.
However, he never tries to change me,
Or tells me how different I could be.
Because he accepts me for what I am,
He's like a lion, while I'm like a lamb.

S Mullinger

Happy 50th Birthday

Today our friend is fifty
He's reached the big five O
We think he is our best friend
And thought we'd tell him so.

He's always been so helpful,
Reliable and true,
If you ring with a problem
He's always there for you.

And so we're pleased to greet him
Upon his special day,
We wish him health and happiness,
Success in every way.

So, have a happy birthday
Whatever you may do,
You're someone very special,
We think the world of you!

Sheila M Gannon

To My Wife

Now she is gone, and I am left:
The light of my life,
My dearest wife,
And I am quite bereft.

She was so full of grace;
Only memories now remain,
Which sometimes give me pain:
But of her there is no trace.

Yet that is not true:
For she still lives on
In that life where she is gone,
Where skies are always blue.

She loved the spring:
The garden with its flowers,
Soft, warm April showers,
And birds on the wing.

For me this truth is glorious -
She is not in a distant land,
But very near at hand;
For she o'er Death is victorious.

How wonderful to know
She is not dead:
Only gone a few short steps ahead,
And one day in her steps I'll follow.

This tribute to my wife I've penned;
It has been such a joy:
For nothing can destroy
Those days ahead together without end.

Kenneth E Jinks

Manuel
(For Manuel Saquic tortured and murdered in Guatemala, 1995)

It's been two years, almost
and these are the first words I've written for you,
my strong brother.
Easter, and we grieve for the crucified,
but all I can see is your body in that unmarked grave.
Oh how you wanted to be found,
holding on and on,
holding in the pain of your thirty-three wounds.
The sky turned black and the temple curtain was torn in two.
The sky turned black and the heavens poured down on you
mixing with the tears,
but the candles did not go out.
And all I can see is your broken body in that unmarked grave,
but the tomb was empty, the stone rolled away
Your tombstone says it all:
      Manuel vive
Only his body lies in this place.

Naomi Young

I Wonder Why

Yesterday will never return
and without you there would have
been no tomorrow.
And today, I wonder why.

I wonder why and what it is
that's trapped you in my heart and mind.
What's so special, what I adore,
what it is in you, I find.

And when I look, deep within,
it's love that's harbouring there.
And when I fell in that deep, dark hole,
you showed me how much you care.

Without you I would never have had the strength
to carry on with life, as I need.
You showed me the way to grab my dreams.
I listened. I heard. I did heed.

And now because of you alone,
because you were there to love,
I'm fighting back, found strength of my own,
you gave me that gentle shove.

I need you in my life, it's true.
Through friendship, you give so much.
There when I need you, to laugh or cry,
there when I need you to touch.

But yesterday will never return,
although I long for the hours we shared.
And there would have been no tomorrow for me,
if you hadn't shown you cared.

And today - I still wonder why.

Jeanette Clinton

My Dear Friend

Sad are my eyes so often,
whenever I think of you.
Knowing time will never return,
but memories stay forever.
Dear trusted friend you were to me.
So many years you shared my joys,
and comforted me in grief.
When I was down in spirits,
you'd always be there for me.
We laughed together many a day,
those were such happy times.
Oh! How those moments sped,
now death has left so much unsaid.
Our earthly paths must part,
Memories of you will never fade,
though sometimes drift into the shade.
Cherished thoughts of you I'll keep forever,
you'll live here always in my heart dear Trevor.

Elisabeth Dill Perrin

Stirling, Edinburgh And Carlisle M8

A motorway humming constantly through
the Venetian blinds of my mind
where washing-up is never dull
and I only torture myself
when a jumper shrinks in the dryer.
The hopeless downer of encompassing passionate
half-light memories erode into
the neon blue of the motorway sign
an absolution for anywhere
and yet, I need not run
for freedom lies with me
entangled in an electric blanket
the duvet of quiet contemplation
against the blackness of oblivion.
Still, clichés come; as clichés do:
'I'd move Stirling, Edinburgh and Carlisle for You!'
On a motorway humming constantly through
the Venetian blinds of my mind
to the service station of my soul.

Nick Brunel

Louise

Most people love the sky
when it is bright and blue
I like it in the early morning
when it is fresh and new
others like it pearly like a shroud
my friend Louise loves it, with puffy cloud

Most people like a garden
when it is straight and neat
I like a garden
full of hidden 'treats'
others like it set in ordered beds
my friend Louise loves flowery 'exotic heads'

Most people would sit
and embroider dainty things
I'd decorate a cloth
with flowers and butterfly wings
others would do items small and twee
my friend Louise does magnificent wall covering tapestry

As you can see
my friend is not like other folk
this I discovered the first time we spoke
her home is 'different' - it's her journey's end
she's 'different'
which is why we're such good friends.

The Painter im Words

Sally Lunn

Contented are we,
Just you and me,
And baby makes three,
In our cottage by the sea,
Rainbow paints the meadow,
But death casts her shadow,
And now I am sad O,
Now I am one,
Babies there are none,
I watch the setting of the sun,
Oh how I loved you Sally Lunn,
You partook in my life,
And I made you my wife,
But now death has won,
The time is now come,
As I sit by the seashore,
Will I see you no more,
You were so full of life and fun,
Where have you gone Sally Lunn,
My hand that took you
Never forsook you,
Now at the ebb of the tide,
I can't describe the pain inside,
So gone are you,
To skies of blue,
But our love's still true,
As sure as a day's journey's done,
I still love you Sally Lunn.

Alan Pow

144

Confirmation

I dreamt that I was crying
Crying like I should of done
That night
Falling into arms that I envisaged
Of which there was none
And it woke me up
Reality, it woke me up

It's a nuisance
Felt better when I was fooling myself
I didn't think it would effect me
It didn't seem to at the time
But I thought you'd be there
Confirm the friendship if I'd seen tears

It's just my insecurity
And pretty much all my fault
Maybe you didn't hear what time I was leaving
Maybe your plate was full
Pure vanity on my part
To expect you there
But anyway
You shouldn't really say goodbye
Or so I've been told

Rebecca Styles

Barbara

So slim and chic with hair so blonde,
As good friends we had grown so fond.
We shared our woes and had our laughs;
Putting the world to rights on everyone's behalf.
She had green fingers, her garden the envy of all,
And baking cakes for all occasions and at everyone's call.
She helped everyone and gave everything of herself,
Until the call from Heaven from the Lord God himself.
As he was to die in pain on the cross,
She took her illness majestically, but to everyone's loss.
My lasting memory was her waving me goodbye,
Giving a half smile, then closing her eyes with a sigh.
One day I hope we will meet once more in Heaven above,
With the flowers she will have planted ready for those she did love.

Valerie Marshall

Roy
(Roy Dixon - RIP)

I'd like to take this chance to say
what everyone here is thinking today
about a man, a truly great friend
who fought the battle for life to the very end.

No gentler milder, person could you find
a man so caring, fun loving and kind
the wonderful way he would smile and say
'How are you keeping, everything okay?'

Not many people can truly declare
that life is for living and just being there
and no one lived life so much to the full
as Roy our friend a fun loving jewel.

We'll never forget his great personal style
of making you welcome to stay for a while
to chat and enquire and hope things were well
and pass on some news, he wished to tell.

Our Lord gave him time to get things sorted out
for his wife and family, which he set about
He blessed each extra day that he was given
and though daily in pain, was thankful for living.

Our thoughts now go out to his family and wife,
we know they've the courage to get on with their life
and we know Roy taught them the way to success
was a cheery 'Hello' with a smile and caress.

We'll miss you Roy.

Robert McFarlane

April 24, 1969
(For Jerry Shriver)

Motorbikes, guitars on fire.
Our teenage life, a youthful game.
In Vietnam, their wading mire,
he disappeared beneath a flame
and no one even spoke his name.

In '69 the headlines scream:
the Woodstock nation, here today.
They're in your face, Utopian dream.
No word, no sound, they didn't say
that Jerry was an MIA.

It's '99, the headlines' fad
is still the same: the rockstar's jeer.
The best of all the best we had
were thrown away. We still don't hear.
Been thirty springtimes, just this year.

Jack Mergott

My Mother

I went to see her place of rest,
It was a cold cold day.
I stood there full of sorrow,
And said a little prayer.

I still hear the church bell ringing,
As if it was yesterday.
When we laid her down to rest,
On that very wet cold day.

Surrounded and yet all alone,
Her body concealed by that polished stone.
I gaze across the holy ground,
So deadly quiet, not a sound.

It's a place we all will visit,
When the Good Lord calls our name.
But I get so sad and lonely,
At my mother lying there.

I know it's in body only,
Her soul has reached on high.
To sit and be with her maker,
In that heaven in the sky.

In our endless search for riches,
We pass each other by.
And all too soon the years they go,
And we watch each other die.

Joe Coleman

An End To Pain
(To the memory of Fred a dear friend)

Please take from me this pain I feel
and ensure me that this isn't real,
that he hasn't gone and left me here
to face the loneliness, the fear.

So from this dream, let me wake tomorrow
and have no need for grief, nor sorrow,
then I will know that he's still there,
to look on me, with love and care.

When I look at him, then I can see
into his eyes that don't see me,
I know it's not a dream, it's real,
please take away the pain I feel

If God can wipe tears from my eyes?
With a promise that the dead will rise,
when we all walk through that special door,
where pain, or death shall be no more.

Colin C Thomas

My Absent Friend

I had a friend, so long ago, a lifetime now it seems,
and he quite often fills my mind, and penetrates my dreams.
We worked on wooden benches then, throughout a lonely day,
and sang old songs, of days gone by, to pass the time away.

Our contest, was about old songs, and which of us knew what,
I'd quote a line, he'd sing a verse, or maybe all the lot.
We delved into our memories, and songs our Mothers sang,
we worked and sang the day away, until the time bell rang.

We were both young, and full of life, those days so long ago,
we each had children, and a wife, and yes! We loved them so.
But tragically our joy was short, like much that's in this life,
when Asian Flu struck down his child, he also lost his wife.

Our friendship stood this test of time, tho' how I'll never know,
our Son was saved, his Daughter lost, and oh! He missed her so.
We still sang songs to pass the time, selected now with care,
our songs were sadder now I fear, for those who were not there.

And so the time went rolling on, an ache replaced the tears,
while sad and dreamy songs of love came ringing down the years.
'Deep in a dream' and 'Blackbird' too, and 'Souvenirs' we'd sing,
all the sad and lonely songs, not those with joyous ring.

The years rolled on, we went our ways, our ladders for to climb,
and each of us, we did quite well! Within our working time.
And tho' I've now lost touch with him, he's half a world away!
I'll think of him, and 'Memories' until my dying day.

Cyril Mepham

Lamentation

*(Dedicated to Paddy Reynolds
who died 1st June 1998)*

Dawn, another morning,
Life, left without warning,
Birds, no longer sing or fly,
Lonely, since you said goodbye.

Noon, half a day gone,
Joy, left too soon,
Clouds, cover the sun,
Rain, no place to run.

Night, empty of you,
Stories, you told so funny and true,
Smiles, you lit in every room,
Sadness, faces full of gloom.

Tears we cry,
Questions why,
You were taken away,
We wanted you to stay.

Lynda Cosgrove

Does Time Heal?

They say time heals
in reality, it only conceals
conceals and hides the truth
for which each loss is a living proof.

When we lose a dear one
we try to turn the page and run
run away, if only for a day
from our sorrow which no words can convey.

I often think I've turned the page
intellectually and sage
thinking that I've overcome the pain
and tomorrow once more will be sane
but alas I only need to hear a certain tune
and out of control quite soon
teardrops cascade upon my cheeks
and depression descends for days and weeks.

It's then I know
sobbing to and fro
that time did not heal
I know because of what I feel.

John O'Sullivan

Happy Childhood Days

Nowadays children grow up so fast; their childhood is gone in a
flash,
And they must have everything that is going whether or no there's
the cash.
But when I recall my childhood years during the Second World War,
We'd no fancy toys or computers, there was no asking for more.

Yet they were wonderful times to have lived, long sunny days spent
outdoors,
And cosy winter nights by the fire, singing songs or helping with the
chores.
We'd the wireless for entertainment, programmes like ITMA and
Have a Go,
To which we listened avidly, hoping the battery would last out the
show!

Sunday evenings were a special time when we'd gather at my
friend's home
To listen to favourite records on their wind-up gramophone,
And her brother would play the piano in his own inimitable style;
I can hear him now, he was so good; the memory brings a smile.

How we revelled in those happy times; how pleasant their memory
yet.
My very good friends and simple needs are things I will never forget.
I can see that children today are happy in their own particular ways,
But I'd say to them 'don't grow up too fast, savour your childhood
days.'

Marlene Allen

154

My So-Called Friend

I had this 'friend'
He was always there
In sun, rain or snow.

I had this 'friend'
He was always bright
And always kept me at bay
For a day.

I had this 'friend'
We used to laugh and play
All day and night
Until he said he'd stay.

I had this 'friend'
Who used to stay every
Friday night
He used to put a bite back
Into my life.

I had this 'friend'
He really was the spice of life
Until one day he cried.

I had this 'friend'
Who announced he was
To wed
I was immediately dead.

I used to have this 'friend'.

Aimée L Webster

155

Remembering Margaret

Oh! How we played as little girls
And how I envied you your curls

We laughed and danced the days away
Our lives were full of fun and play

As teenagers we worked apart
Awaiting adult life to start

The days of wartime passed, like sorrows
And then began our real tomorrows

Came romance, love and pledges given
We'd made the leap from girls to women

I was your bridesmaid - you were mine
Our friendship stood the test of time

We both had sons you three, me one
And somehow carefree days were gone

Yet still those childhood memories bound us
With loving families around us

Then grandchildren brought their special love
Each one bequeathed a treasure trove

We'd meet and sip a friendly cup
Wondering how we'd become 'grown-up'

Then you became ill - how could this be
You were the one who was younger than me

But you were still my dearest friend
We cherished our memories right to the end

Now I still see your smiling face
And remember your gentleness and grace

You'll always be that laughing girl
My loving friend with the bouncing curls

Peggy Smith

Penny

Your hair, raven black
In Celtic interlacing often held
And shining under sun or silver moon.
Nothing does it lack.
Your eyes, dark and deep
Yet as bright as your flashing smile
And warm and gentle without any guile.
Peacefully do you sleep.
Sometimes you are still,
Quiet and serious, thinking very hard.
Sometimes you are joyful and excited
And you laugh at will.
Your mouth is satin soft
And generous, used to patient talk.
Your skin, fresh flower fragrant scent
Like fruit-filled wine quaffed.
You know your own mind -
You are determined and have many gifts
Like the wife of Ulysses at heart,
Courageous and kind.
You like to play the game
Of life, of work, of travel, rest and love.
You have uncounted riches deep within
Though Penny is your name.

Robin Kiel

A Birthday Card

1906 was a memorable year
A year when 'character' was born.
Good fairies at your cradle
indomitable spirit of youth bestowed.

Too young to fight
the war to end all wars
which festered on
a second war to spawn,
in which you served your country valiantly.

And through it all,
the butterflies of life
light gently on the works that you create.
With artistry of pen and brush,
imagination you do titillate.

God gave you many gifts.
Good steward that you are,
in all the abundance that he gave,
nothing is wasted,
nothing lost.
The talent for loving, sharing, caring
has blessed the lives of all who all you 'Friend'.

Dear James at ninety-two
you're far too young
to ever think of growing old.

Janet White Spunner

159

Remembering Mum

(In loving memory of Maureen Winifred Waddup
22.10.1936-19.5.1997, always loved, never forgotten)

She was a warm and caring person
Loved by her three daughters and one son
A true lady was she, with dignity and charm
No matter how annoyed she got, she always stayed so calm

Through the years that we shared she showed us what life was about
We never wanted for anything, although she often went without
Now we've all grown up and families we have of our own
Our children we guide through life, just as once we were shown

Dad remembers when you were both young and carefree
You was the pretty girl that he was to marry
You was more than a lover, you were also his best friend
How sad it is, for all good things come to an end

With you dad shared the best forty years
Stories of you and him, with us he now shares
We hear the emotion filling in his voice
For his love he has lost, but not by choice

Pam Culverhouse

The Silent World
(For my granddaughter Ayesha who is profoundly deaf)

The children who love in the silent world
Do not complain
For they can see colours, sense speech
And feel the rain
The children who live in the silent world
Show their love
They know kindness, smell flowers
And know God above.

The children who live in the silent world
Are strong in heart
Their faith endures, their insight inspires
They play their part
The children who live in the silent world
Will always be your friend
Their actions touch you, you are not afraid
Their love has no end.

So for the children of the silent world
Hold out your arms
Gather them in as roses, hold them close
Cause them no harm.
Give you love to a child in the silent world
Your voice is their song
Keep the door to your heart open, hold out your hand
Help them, as they travel along.

Margaret Gurney

Friendship

Friendship is something that's hard to find,
When found it should be treated as precious,
For this closeness is worth its weight in gold,
And no other situation can match it.

A friend is someone who eases your pain,
Makes you see that your life means so much,
They make you happy when you're feeling down,
Whenever you need them they're there.

With a friend you can always rely on them,
To come out with the right words,
They always know the best things to say,
You miss them when they're not around.

Being with your friend means you strengthen the bond,
That allows you simply to be,
Nothing should ever come between friends,
For friendship is you and me.

Sarah Findlay

Intensity

I am so hurt, have lost my way
Frightened for the morrow and
Damned to-day.
What experience to be gained so?
Why such hardships? It's best to know.
One is maimed by the pain of life
The slings and arrows, and the knife.
Oh! For one who is kind
Yet cruel, the pressing touch
Of a spiritual breath . . .
Or to grip the warmth of wool
On a fevant chest.
Just for a minute let me stay:
You have already walked this way . . .

L P P

Louise
(On her first birthday)

Your smile is full of sunshine,
Your laughter's full of song
That's tuned to love and beauty,
To help each day along.

Your toes are full of movement,
Your dainty fingers too,
We think you'll be a dancer,
We're all so proud of you.

Your big blue eyes - they twinkle
And shine so good and true.
As you grow up, we pray
Life will be good to you.

Your face is full of innocence,
A little mischief too.
We're grateful you were sent to us,
Thank God he gave us you.

Joanne Quinton

For Better Or Verse . . .

You're beer 'n darts,
I'm Oxford and wine.
You hate the Arts,
And I like to dine.

Our differences are bizarre,
At odds with all around.
But you're special the way you are.
And tied to you I'm bound.

Jackie Callow

Adolescence Remembered

It only seems like yesterday,
When problems were miles away.
The fun we had, the joy we shared,
We thought for life, we were prepared.
Wigan Casino, the Rugby Club,
A friendship that was oh so good.
Sharing school days, heart to heart,
Not many days, were we apart.
We shared the laughter and the tears,
All throughout our teenage years,
No friendship could compare to ours,
Blessed by God's almighty powers.
A partnership to compliment,
To share the gifts that we'd been sent.
Memories to make us smile,
When we haven't met, in quite a while.
I remember you, my friend with love.
For you were sent by God above.
You blessed my life and taught me much.
To fond memories, my heart does clutch.
For now as women, we have grown.
Each of us, has her own home.
Children have enriched our days,
Contented us, in many ways.
At this special time, I think of you,
Send you greetings warm and true.
I close my eyes and I recall,
You were the greatest friend, of all.

Janet Parry

When You Passed Away

When you passed away, I was sad
that day, yet happy
your suffering had ended.
A little white dove, came from above
just as the Lord intended.

Your last few weeks in a
hospital bed would not have been
to your choosing.
The man above was being unfair
did he know what we were losing?

A Gran with a heart so loving and fair
A Gran who had given so much
A Gran who always understood
And always was in touch.

Your health is your wealth
you used to say, look after it whilst you're here
and if there's enough food, to feed
the brood; it will stand you
in good cheer.

Brown bread you baked, I smell it still,
post office and savings for us
a fish and chip supper as a treat you liked
you were never one to fuss

Nineteen eighty-three it was, when
you went to the other side
I stood around your graveside,
sad; but full of pride.

To have known someone so special
is a privilege you know,
and your ring, I wear it every day
and everywhere I go.

These words I write
with some delight, now having
a chance to say, how much
you really meant to me,
and still do to this day.

Don Meehan

Bygones
(For Mary-Jane)

I wish that I'd been there for you
to share your pain, and help you through.
To lend an ear, and lend a hand,
when other folks don't under-stand.

The words and wishes, often sent,
from peo-ple full of good intent.
Some groan, and say 'Ooh, I've got a pain,'
and you think to yourself huh, think again.'

Your wish is not to seem un-caring,
but they don't feel half of what you're bearing.
So you breath a sym-pa-thetic blow
and you listen to their tales of woe.

Then you sit them down and make a dash,
to the place of your me-dicinal stash.
You give them two-aspirin and a cup-of-tea
and think 'Christ, I wish that would work for me'.

I'm sure your family stand-by-you,
but there isn't much that they can do.
And there's little I can do-or-say,
to make your suffering go-away.

Well now that we're in-touch-again,
I'm here-for-you when you're-in-pain.
Don't sit and suffer si-lent-ly,
I know what it's like, believe-you-me.

So if you're suff-ering, don't despair,
just think of me, and I'll be there.
As I said, I'm not a miracle man,
but I'll try and do-the-best-I-can.

G P Garoghan

Just Another Sad, Sad Parting

And now it's over, no hidden disgrace,
Just a drifting apart, no vicious words.
A kiss on the cheek without fond embrace;
Is this how feelings end, no crossing swords?

Each knowing years of good marriage and love,
Losing loved ones by death, meeting by chance,
No thought that age might a divider prove,
Friendship blossomed, without need of romance.

Learning to share our friendship together,
The years passed by with both pleasure and joy,
True to each other, few thoughts of whether
Time would soon part us, its forces deploy.

Partings come in different coloured cloaks,
Much memory stays, future now is hopes.

Edgar Wall

Little Friends

I have two very special friends,
Nicola and Richard by name,
At birth they were brain injured,
so you see they are both the same,
Nicola I've know for some nine years,
and little Richard for well over five,
These two young kids need so much help,
and to raise funds for them I strive.

Upwell, Cambs, is Richard's home,
Nicola's from Jarrow, Tyne and Wear,
yet despite the problems in their lives,
they always smile and show good cheer,
Both go to schools for special needs,
where they are taught to work and play,
For me it's now a big part of my life,
raising funds for my two friends each day.

To see Nicola and Richard's progress,
fills me with much pride and joy,
I remember them in their early years,
just a rag doll type little girl and boy,
Myself, I spend life in a wheelchair,
and good friends I have many indeed,
These friends give me encouragement,
to ensure that my work will succeed,
Friendship is important, sharing others' strife,
for Nicola and Richard; it's helping them in life.

Wenn The Penn

The Memorial

Preserved in time and granite page,
No lines of life or care can ever
  mark your brow or single you in
  rage.

The inexplicable hand of Fate decreed
  that you would ne'er be sage
Nor suffer the vicissitudes that come
  with age.

Now Old Majority arrives upon you in
  another place -
A better place, perchance.

Await us at the crossroads of the heart
  and soul -
An appointment we must keep some weird
  and unavoidable date.

Know us when we come,
As we have known you on each partially
  empty day since you have gone.

Inked in your memoriam of twenty-one.

  Charles Mullally

Fun In Our Cul-De-Sac

It seems like only yesterday
  That we were young and free.
Skipping and laughing in the sun,
  Happy and so carefree.
Mothers chatting by their doors,
  No traffic to disturb us then.
'Whoops' I tell a lie
  Sometimes we had to lower the rope
(To let a cart go by).
  Times seemed always sunny then
Though we did not mind the rain,
  For when it spluttered in the gutter
We played our favourite game.
  An empty matchbox, a paper boat
What fun to see them float.
  Tossing our shoes and socks aside
We paddled in the rain.
  Blocked-up drains did not trouble us then
It helped us play this game.
  Alas! Those carefree days are gone
With all my childhood friends
  Never to return again.

Vee Smith

Anne
(For my friend, Anne Reilly)

Walled up in my loneliness,
afraid of breaking free
from my self-imposed prison,
I tried to make sense of madness
around me and within.

Then along came Anne,
with that glorious auburn hair
and such merry laughing eyes.
She had a warm compassionate heart,
my funny lovely Anne.

Slowly my prison walls gave way,
persuaded by her friendship and her love.
The arid world, much watered by my tears,
transformed into a garden,
beautified by smiles.

Anne will never know perhaps
how much she meant to me,
so lost and ill at ease with life.
The way was difficult sometimes,
with memories not always kind.

So many faces come and go,
pass through the teeming mind,
yet time nor tide can ever take
her image from this heart of mine,
my brave, my bright haired Anne.

Megan Guest

Requiem For Marianne

Somewhere her slender bones may lie
Or, carried by the wind, perhaps her dust
Is merging with the alien earth
Of her adopted land. Nothing else
Of her brief and bitter life is left
Except her voice that in silence sounds
Only in the stillness of my mind
And the recollected touch of hands
Falling light on my waiting arm.
Time has no meaning now for her:
She is one with the ageless dark;
One with the long past;
Closer now the ancient dead
Than to her shadow lingering still
In the uncertain shelter of my love.
I cannot mourn her chosen death:
The last release was welcome when it came.
I only grieve because the hours
That sped her footsteps to the dark
Could not provide, with all my love,
Enough for her to want to stay,
And wherever her bones may lie
Or where her scattering dust may fall,
My love shall be her monument,
My memories her pall.

Geoffrey Page

Rollercoaster

Slowly patiently, working together
Finding in each other a meaning to life
Hurtling to the top together they flew
seeking the hiatus given to few

Looking at love in a different way
Finding joy in every new day
Living together on the mountain top
of life with the privileged ones

Falling swiftly, now at the bottom
of the deepest trough that life can find
seeking the answers in life's thick mire
Knowing not where to turn but into themselves

Tumbling towards the inevitable end
Turning all ways for just one true friend
Climbing again up the steep incline
of life's natural hills and keeping in time
with the ups and the downs of their spiritual minds

Love's happy feelings swinging them high
Love's lowest ebbs wondering why
they try to combine love and life together as one
when all will be taken away on a tidal wave
of suspicion a whirlwind of distrust

The rollercoaster of life has them in its grip
making hearts jump causing stomachs to flip
Now they are down now they climb up
Where will they find a straight road to follow
but in the friendship that makes all things well

Fiona Higgins

Remembering Friends

Have to remember all that have meet
Even the bookie who tell can't beat
Can remember the seven within barn
Thousands came towards us yet no harm
We take chance for world and Great Britain
Got pushed so quickly, not wanted smitten
The friends all made remember short time
Those that we lost got more honour fine
Have made many more over the long years
Some have now gone, feel the swell of tears

But each day meet more who ask for hand
Still remembering years flying life was grand
Some state they have only voted country one
Perhaps because no education only poor dunce
Didn't have funds but so many real good friends
Others tried to twist the finance to meet the ends
If had chance would do the same again for fun
Am now too old no jogging can't even do long run
Only the council seem to want put me down under
When look at some of them must look like thunder

Full life have lived could just write for ever more
More friends than Great Britain has thing called law
Never wanted double pay was satisfied with wage
Still remember when started was so happy be page
In rectory went to church with the best in young years
Often wonder what happened curate loved to cheers
Sorry can't travel so fast now because of my age
But fit in with the ordinary people forget the rage
The people in this world have made what I am
Being their friend much better than smoked ham.

J J Flint

Brenda

I miss her laughter and the cheerful soul of her,
Especially the smiles that covered her despair
When care o'erwhelmed her nearly, yet could not destroy
Her love of life, her sense of fun, the inner joy
That kept her going day by day. We shared so much.

We went to concerts, candlelit Vivaldi and Mozart;
She loved romantic things, red roses and fine art.
Mimicry and anecdote were all a part of her;
For all these precious things, I will remember her.

We chanted scraps of verse, remembered from schooldays,
Recalled old songs and quoted favourite Shakespeare plays,
The books we'd read that filled our girlish heads with dreams,
Bewailed our long-lost youth (how far away it seems).
She was my soul-mate and she had that magic touch!

Her passing leaves me desolate, she was a friend
And nothing tangible is left but memories, that bend
And sadly fade 'neath Time's relentless hand,
But she is free and Time may help me understand.

Betty Winbolt

A Broken Link
(In memory of Joyce)

My heart is heavy, my eyes are red
For a dear friend my tears are shed
Her daughter wrote to say that she
Had passed away just recently

Oh she was special, earned my tears
Best friend through many teenage years
And even with five decades gone
The memories still linger on

Inseparable for years on end
No one could want a better friend
We shared our secrets and our dreams
Our schoolwork, sweets and magazines

Together at the Saturday dance
Each hoping we would find romance
Then next week four of us would go
To the local picture show

Our adult lives went different ways
And work and families filled our days
But still we met now and again
And always said 'Remember when . . .?'

For years we both lived miles apart
But love for her stayed in my heart
We often wrote and phoned but still
She didn't tell me she was ill

Now that link has gone at last
No more will we relive the past
I'm sad, but glad she's free from pain
And, please God, we shall meet again.

Audrey Gunnill

Iona

Small girl with enormous blue eyes full of wonder
Her forehead the unknowing plain against which waves
Crash their bright charge on the cliff face and ebb away
Back into an ocean of other confusion.
With clusters of thrifty sharp utterances from
Tiny rose lips in the chalk white circumference.
Rock pools of possibility dimplement her
Cheeks happily innocent in their jest.
Her pert lighthouse nose stands prominently
On a terrace of chalky facial hair
So soft that you hardly dare kiss its yield
On the firm flesh it spring from. By contrast
Hebridean tousles sprout deep jungles
Of ever flowing curls to sweep strange dark
Intrigue on shoulders of half formed human,
Untiring in her quest for mystery.

K Plumb

Happy Father's Day
(This poem is dedicated to my father, Ray O'Dowd)

Happy Father's Day, Dad.
I hope you'll be glad with the day
You will have.
Happy Father's Day, Dad.
Keep looking at the sky for your
Rainbow green, orange, yellow and
Blue and when you do, follow its end,
And I hope you will find your pot of
Gold with all the love you ever could
Hold.

Caroline O'Dowd (10)